CW00501658

A Goodly Heritage a Simple Church History

Georgiana M. Forde

BIBLIOLIFE

Copyright © BiblioLife, LLC

BiblioLife Reproduction Series: Our goal at BiblioLife is to help readers, educators and researchers by bringing back in print hard-to-find original publications at a reasonable price and, at the same time, preserve the legacy of literary history. The following book represents an authentic reproduction of the text as printed by the original publisher and may contain prior copyright references. While we have attempted to accurately maintain the integrity of the original work(s), from time to time there are problems with the original book scan that may result in minor errors in the reproduction, including imperfections such as missing and blurred pages, poor pictures, markings and other reproduction issues beyond our control. Because this work is culturally important, we have made it available as a part of our commitment to protecting, preserving and promoting the world's literature.

All of our books are in the "public domain" and some are derived from Open Source projects dedicated to digitizing historic literature. We believe that when we undertake the difficult task of re-creating them as attractive, readable and affordable books, we further the mutual goal of sharing these works with a larger audience. A portion of BiblioLife profits go back to Open Source projects in the form of a donation to the groups that do this important work around the world. If you would like to make a donation to these worthy Open Source projects, or would just like to get more information about these important initiatives, please visit www.bibliolife.com/opensource.

A Goodly Heritage

A SIMPLE CHURCH HISTORY

BY

GEORGIANA M. FORDE

With Preface by the Rev.

CANON BENHAM, D.D.

Rector of St Edmund the King, London.

"I speak concerning Christ and the Church"—Eph. v. 32
that ye may
"Be ready always to give an answer to every man that asketh you,
a reason of the hope that is in you."—1 S. Peter iii. 15.

THIRD EDITION

London

SKEFFINGTON & SON

34 SOUTHAMPTON STREET, STRAND, W.C.

Publishers to His Majesty The King

1903

PREFACE

THE MS. of this little volume was put into my hands, on behalf of the Authoress, by the widow of one who still bears an honoured name in the Church. I read it through and entirely agree with her that it is well worthy of publication. For, indeed, I do not know another work which is so likely to win the attention of the young, or to give them a true notion of what the Catholic Church is, or what a bright future lies before the English branch of it, by the blessing of Almighty God. I should like to know that the book has been adopted in Sunday Schools, and that its successive heads are expanded by the teachers who are rising up, and who, according to my own experience, are showing ever more and more attachment to the faith of Christ Crucified. So much that I have seen of late has moved me to 'thank God and take courage.'

Here and there I have made a few suggestions which I have reason to hope have pleased her. But the book is her own, one clear definite idea, with which I am entirely in agreement with her, running through it. I have never seen her, but I delight in her book and thank her for it.

WILLIAM BENHAM.

CONTENTS

CHAP.		PAGE
I.	The Church's Birthday—The One Baptism—Story of Genes—Confirmation	1
II.	Nero's Persecution—Martyrdom of S. Peter and S. Paul, of S. Ignatius and S. Polycarp—The Catacombs—Martyrdom of S. Sixtus and S. Lawrence	11
III.	Glastonbury Abbey—Romans conquer Britain—The Thundering Legion—S. Alban . .	29
IV.	Fall of Rome—Picts and Scots harass the Britons—S. Germanus and the Hallelujah Battle—The Saxons—Lives of S. Patrick and S. Columba	42
V.	S. Gregory and English Slaves—S. Augustine sent to England—British Church remains independent—S. Paulinus	60
VI.	Oswald, King and Saint—S. Aidan—Synod of Whitby—Hilda and Caedmon—Life of the Venerable Bede	79
VII.	The Coming of the Danes—King Alfred—Martyrdom of S. Alphege—Edward the Confessor .	95
VIII.	The Normans — Wulfstan, Saxon Bishop of Worcester — Osmund and "The Use of Sarum" — Anselm and Henry — Death of Thomas Becket, Archbishop of Canterbury—King John and Stephen Langton . . .	106

Contents

CHAP.		PAGE
IX.	Roman demands resisted by Grosseteste—The Crusades — Wycliffe translates the Bible—Luther and the Reformation abroad—Henry VIII. suppresses the Monasteries . . .	122
X.	The English Church casting away Roman Error—Edward VI. and the Protector Somerset—Queen Mary restores Romanism—Elizabeth again overthrows the Pope's Power in England	132
XI.	James I. and the Authorised Version of the Bible—Death of Archbishop Laud and of Charles I.—Cromwell suppresses the Prayer Book—Restoration of Charles II. and the Church's Public Services—James II. and the Seven Bishops—William of Orange and the Non-Jurors	141
XII.	The Preaching of John and Charles Wesley—The Wesleyans at the Present Time—The Salvation Army—The Church's Care of the Young and Sick and Wandering — The Church founded and preserved by Christ will last till His Appearing	150

INTRODUCTION

WHO founded THE CHURCH?

Not a man, not an angel even.

It was Jesus Christ, our Saviour, who founded the Christian Church.

He has cared for her for nineteen hundred years, and He will watch over her, till the Church Militant on earth, and the Church Expectant in Paradise, shall be merged into the Church Triumphant in Heaven, that happy place where she shall be safe for ever.

Our Lord was forty days on earth between His rising from the dead on Easter Day and His going up to Heaven on Ascension Day—the Great Forty Days they are called: a most mysterious time.

Suddenly He would appear through closed doors, and as suddenly vanish. On the seashore, on a mountain, during a walk, while the disciples were sitting at a meal, He would miraculously show Himself, and miraculously disappear.

We know very little of the exact words He spoke on these occasions, but S. Luke mentions that He talked "of the things pertaining to the Kingdom of God," which means the Church.

On Ascension Day He went up into Heaven, and on Whitsunday sent down, as He promised, the Holy Spirit, bringing life to the Church, knitting its members together into one living body, leading the Apostles into all truth, teaching them all things, and bringing all things to their remembrance, whatsoever Jesus had said unto them.

Accordingly we find the Apostles not at all puzzled as to how the Church was to be managed after Jesus Christ had left them, and one doing one thing and one another. Calmly and orderly they baptized, confirmed, and ordained Bishops, Priests, and Deacons, to carry on the work after they should die, and from that day to ours the blessed work of the Church has been going on without a break.

Christ is gone up, yet ere He passed
From earth in Heaven to reign,
He formed one Holy Church to last
Till He should come again.

His Twelve Apostles first He made
  His ministers of grace ;
And they their hands on others laid
  To fill in turn their place.

So age by age, and year by year
  Christ's grace is handed on ;
And still the Holy Church is here,
  Although her Lord is gone.

Let those find pardon, Lord, from Thee
  Whose love to her is cold ;
Bring wanderers in, and let there be
  One Shepherd, and one fold.

AMEN.

How glad we ought to be that we are members of Christ's ancient glorious Church.

Jesus Himself is our Head, and the Saints of all ages are our companions, for you know we say in our Creed, "I believe in the Communion of Saints." Communion means sharing in common, or, joining together, the joining of all Christian people into Christ's great family.

Some members of the family have long passed away, but though separated in body from us by death, their spirits still live, and they still form part of Christ's family. We should think of them as we do of our earthly relations who are living in distant lands, such as India or America.

We do not see them, but we remember them, they still are our relations and dear to us, and we hope one day to meet them again.

And surely enough, one day, the Great Resurrection Day, all the members of Christ's family will meet again ; "the dead in Christ shall rise first," then the saints who are still living on the earth "shall be caught up together with them in the clouds to meet the Lord in the air, and so shall we ever be with the Lord," Christ's glorious Church Triumphant.

A Goodly Heritage

CHAPTER I

The Church's Birthday—The One Baptism—Story of Genes—Confirmation

"Except a man be born of water, and of the Spirit, he cannot enter into the Kingdom of God."

ON Ascension Day our Lord Jesus Christ went up into Heaven. He told His disciples that this was really for their good, "For if I go not away, the Comforter will not come unto you, but if I depart I will send Him unto you."

The disciples had only ten days to wait for this priceless gift. Then came a great Feast of the Jews, the Day of Pentecost. Our Prayer Book name for it is Whitsunday.

The little band of believers in our Lord were assembled together, most likely in that upper room where Jesus had instituted the Sacrament of the Holy Communion seven weeks before.

"Suddenly there came a sound from Heaven as of a rushing mighty wind, and it filled all the house where they were sitting."

More marvellous still, tongues, or flames of fire, rested on the head of each of the Apostles, "and they were all filled with the Holy Ghost and began to speak with other tongues." The foreign Jews who were at Jerusalem then for the Feast came together in a multitude, and "were all amazed, and marvelled, saying one to another, Behold, are not all these which speak Galileans? And how hear we every man in our own tongue wherein we were born." And good news it was they heard. The Crucified Jesus was their Risen Saviour, and if they repented and were baptized, they too should receive the Holy Ghost.

That was the Church's Birthday; and on it God gave her many costly presents, for we read, "Then they that gladly received his" (S. Peter's) "word were baptized, and the same day there were added unto them about three thousand souls!" This gift of the Holy Ghost knitted them together into one living body, the Church.

And that same Holy Spirit does indeed come to us also in a special manner when we are baptized.

I do not mean that He gives us power to speak strange languages. Such powers were the *Extraordinary Gifts* of the Holy Ghost, as they are called, and they are not needed in this age of the Church as they were at first.

But we do get in abundance the *Ordinary Gifts* of the Holy Ghost, and by them quite as wonderful things are wrought.

I was at a friend's house in Kilburn a few years ago, and I heard there a young English missionary, Mr G. W. Brooke, who had just come from Africa, tell what miracles God's Holy Spirit had worked among the savage tribe he had been living with.

When he first went to them they used to kill each other on the slightest provocation, and they were terrible to their sick. If any one of their relations, whether parent or child even, fell ill, they dug a hole deep enough to bury the invalid up to his neck, and there he was left to die in slow torture, with poisonous insects stinging his face and a fierce sun beating down on his unprotected head. No one was allowed to bring even a drop of water to the poor sufferer under pain of sharing the same ghastly fate.

After a time, however, these cannibals began to listen to the missionary telling them about their Great Father, God, who loved them so much, and who gave His dear Son to save them and His Holy Spirit to make them gentle and kind, and Who was sorely grieved when they did these cruel things.

Gradually one wicked custom was given up and then another, and now these very men who were such awful murderers are living lives that would put to shame many a Christian in this land.

It was God's Holy Spirit alone that caused this stupendous change,—the very same Comforter who was given to the Church that first Whitsunday and has been with her ever since.

Surely you must acknowledge that His work now is as marvellous as in the Apostles' time: His *Ordinary Gifts* as precious as His *Extraordinary* ones.

After receiving the outpouring of the Holy Spirit the Apostles were told to deliver the Gospel (the good spell or speech is the meaning of the word) first to the Jews; but as they rejected and crucified the Lord Jesus, so they rejected the Church He founded and tried their best to ruin it.

They stoned S. Stephen to death, and then Herod "killed James the brother of John with the sword," and we are told that this "pleased the Jews."

The Apostles were beaten and imprisoned, and forbidden to speak in the name of Jesus; but instead of being terrified, they rejoiced at being allowed the honour of suffering for Him, and they confessed Him before men all the more bravely and earnestly.

Persecution also helped to spread the Faith, for the disciples finding they were being hunted down in Jerusalem, and remembering their Master's words, "when they persecute you in this city, flee ye into another," escaped to the neighbouring countries, and wherever they went they preached Christ and enrolled members into His Church by Baptism.

This sacrament of Baptism is the entrance into the Church, and it is so necessary, that the lowest order in the Christian ministry, the deacons, may baptize, and when there is great danger, and no time to fetch a clergyman, anyone may baptize.

I have seen in the Church of S. Michael and All Angels, Sydenham, a Register of Baptisms, and one of the entries was this:—"April 26th 1885. Ellen Louisa . . . privately baptized in the absence of a lawful minister by F. D. Hamilton." He was the doctor attending the baby, and believing it to be dying fast, he baptized it, and in the Church's books it is recorded as a true baptism.

It very rarely happens however in England, that a clergyman cannot be found close at hand to bestow "the means of grace."

Still, as many of you may go out to our distant Colonies, where clergy and churches are only planted here and there, it is quite possible that you may have to administer the Sacrament of Baptism to some dying person — then remember that if you use water and the Name of the Holy Trinity, such Baptism will be accepted by God on high, and His Church on earth.

There is a story you might like to hear of a heathen clown called Genes who lived in the days of the persecuting Emperor Diocletian, about 300 years after Christ was born.

Genes had continually to be finding new ways of entertaining the Emperor and his Court, and as he knew they hated the Christians, he used to hold them up to ridicule and raise many a laugh about their ways of living.

One day he thought he would act a mock baptism, so he had a tub of water brought on to the stage, and he dressed up his assistant clown like a clergyman and then showed him what he was to do.

"You must pour water over my head and say at the same time, 'Genes, I baptize thee in the Name of the Father, and of the Son, and of the Holy Ghost.'"

The assistant obeyed these instructions exactly, and as Genes lifted up his head with the drops of water still glistening on it, the people expected they should hear some of his witty blasphemy against the new religion of the Crucified One; but Genes never spoke; instead, he looked far away beyond the amphitheatre, high up in the deep blue sky, as if he saw something most wonderful there.

The spectators only thought this was part of the performance and that he was acting a devout Christian admirably.

"First-rate, Genes, first-rate, my boy, you have just caught their mawkish look," was shouted in applause.

Still Genes never spoke.

The Emperor on his gilded throne sent to know what was the matter, and Genes was brought before him.

"My lord Augustus," he said in low tones, "I am speaking the truth: at the time the water was poured on me, I saw a bright light and Angels were about me. Hitherto I have mocked the Christians, now I confess that I too believe in their Jesus Christ."

"Genes, you are beside yourself, or ill, to utter such words before me; go home and rest," replied the Emperor, reprovingly.

"My lord, I am a Christian," persisted the clown, "I am indeed."

Diocletian then became angry and ordered in "the little horse," a horrible instrument of torture. "A touch of that will soon cure his folly," he said.

That torture was endured and others too, but nothing shook the faith of the newly-baptized Christian.

Before the sun set that day Genes had received the Crown of Martyrdom, the executioner's sword at length releasing his ransomed soul.

One warning I must give you about Baptism—never, never must you allow yourself to be "baptized twice." If you have been baptized as a baby, you have obeyed God's command, and you would sorely grieve His Holy Spirit if you went again through the form of Baptism. It would really not be a Baptism at all.

There is "One Lord, One Faith, One Baptism." Our Lord Jesus speaks of Baptism as being "born again." Of course you know it is impossible for a child to be *born* twice in a bodily shape on the earth, and it is just as impossible for the same soul to be *born* twice into the Heavenly Kingdom. So there can be but one Baptism.

Confirmation is the next important step in the Christian life; alas! not all who have begun well by Baptism come on to this.

I asked a woman once why she would not be confirmed and she said there was nothing about it in the Bible!

For fear any others may think like her I advise them to read for themselves the account of the first Confirmation, when S. Peter and S. John went down to Samaria to confirm the converts that S. Philip the deacon had baptized. It is found in the eighth chapter of the Acts of the Apostles. "Then laid they their hands on them and they received the Holy Ghost." In our Prayer Book too, you will find the other name for Confirmation is "The Laying-on of Hands."

It is the same to-day as in S. Philip's time. Priests and deacons may baptize, but have not power to confirm. It is only the Bishops, the successors of the Apostles, who may "lay their hands" on the candidates, and thus confirm them.

All who come to "years of discretion" are not only missing a great blessing, but also are neglecting their duty, unless they come to Confirmation.

There is so little we can do for the Lord Jesus who has done so much for us, but we can do this one thing for Him. At Confirmation we stand up before the congregation, and boldly confess "the faith of Christ crucified;" that He is our God, by our own free choice; and that we do mean, and try, to live for His glory. That is our part of the rite.

But God's part is far weightier. He welcomes His sons and daughters, and gives them again the same Holy Spirit that He did in Baptism, but this time in sevenfold might; for it is ever His way to give according as we are able to receive.

Strengthened and purified by this outpouring of the Holy Spirit, we are permitted to draw near with faith, and take the greatest blessing that is ours on earth — the Communion of Christ's Body and Blood, to which those who are now confirmed may come, and there may "taste, and see, how gracious the Lord is"!

CHAPTER II

Nero's Persecution—Martyrdom of S. Peter and S. Paul, of S. Ignatius and S. Polycarp—The Catacombs—Martyrdom of S. Sixtus and S. Lawrence

"In the world ye shall have tribulation."

JUST before the Lord Jesus went up into Heaven, He gave this command to His disciples, "Go ye into all the world, and preach the Gospel to every creature," a command still strongly laid on His Church, for alas! though 1900 years have rolled by since He uttered these words, there are yet quite half of the inhabitants of this earth who have never even heard of the mighty Saviour who has redeemed them. If we cannot go out personally as missionaries we must do our utmost in other ways to help the Church to carry the message of love to the heathen that they may be turned from darkness to light, or else we are neglecting to obey this our Lord's last command.

Nowadays it is no easy task to convert the heathen, but in the Apostles' time it was far more difficult.

The Romans were then masters of the whole known world, and you must remember that their punishment for the lowest sort of criminals was crucifixion, as degrading as hanging is with us. Yet the Creed of Christians is to believe in a Crucified Saviour and to glory in the Cross; and this was what the Apostles had to tell these proud conquerors.

How they would mock!

Remember too, how sunk in wickedness the nations were then. No one was ashamed of leading an impure or selfish life; sin was openly committed by rich and poor.

No hospitals were to be seen anywhere for the sick and old. It was Christianity that built them later.

Human life was counted very cheap. Men, women and children were bought and sold and became the absolute property of their owners, who might ill-treat them, or put them to death as they liked. It will give you an idea of how they were treated when I tell you that three kinds of property were recognized—the "speaking, the half speaking, and the dumb." You will hardly guess what these three meant. The "speaking" were the slaves, the "half speaking," were the animals, and the "dumb" were tables and chairs and such-like furniture! It was Christ who showed that the slave was equal with his master in being created by God, and made in His likeness.

Very cruel were people then, not only with their slaves but in every way. To see human suffering was an excitement and pleasure; and the chief amusement of Rome, the greatest city in the world, was to watch gladiators or professional fighters kill each other in the Colosseum, as their gigantic theatre was called, or wrestle with savage lions or leopards, until they were torn to pieces.

To such men as these, the Gospel of peace, and goodwill, and forgiveness was to be preached.

How *could* the Apostles, how dared they, preach it?

They could, and they did, with marvellous success, too, but only by the help of that Holy Spirit, who is ever with the Church.

A few years afterwards, when the awful persecutions began, their converts proved by their steadfastness how thoroughly they had accepted the Crucified One as indeed the true Son of God, their Saviour. For this Faith they were ready to give up all that the world holds pleasant and lovely, and even to lay down life itself.

The first persecution was, of course, that which followed the stoning of S. Stephen, but it did not go beyond the land of Syria.

Roughly speaking, there were ten general persecutions before Christianity became the established religion of the Roman Empire under Constantine.

God's "noble army of Martyrs" did wonders for Him at these times.

Bishops, slaves, grey-headed men and women, strong lads and quite little children, died painful deaths for love of Jesus.

S. Symeon, the second Bishop of Jerusalem, was 120 years old when he was crucified, while S. Cyriacus had barely reached his third summer when the cruel prefect of Tarsus ended the short life by dashing him on to the stone pavement of the judgment hall.

In those days Christians were made the scapegoats on whom the blame for every calamity was laid; whether earthquake, famine, plague, or war, they were said to have caused it, and were at once hunted out so that the discontent of the mob might be visited on them.

The Emperor Nero declared that his great persecution was to punish the Christians for having set fire to Rome. Of course they had never done such a thing; indeed, it was commonly whispered that the Emperor himself had caused the conflagration on purpose, that he might rebuild the city on a more magnificent scale.

On this occasion the martyrs' clothes were soaked in pitch or oil, then they were placed on pedestals in the Imperial Parks, and at a given time were set on fire, so as to illuminate the walks with living candles. In a far deeper sense than Nero ever dreamt of, they did let their light shine before men!

Other tortures were also devised, such as wrapping Christians in the skins of wild beasts, and then throwing them to savage dogs to be worried to death.

S. Peter and S. Paul both suffered martyrdom under the Emperor Nero, a monster of iniquity, who had dared to murder even his own mother.

I must explain here that the Romans, as a rule, tolerated the religions of the countries they conquered, and even built temples for them. Why then did they so fiercely persecute Christ's followers?

Well, one reason was, that they could not understand the largeness of Christianity. It was not the particular religion of one state or people. "I believe in the Holy Catholic Church" was, and is, the Creed of every true disciple of Jesus, whatever part of the world he may be living in.

Now Catholic means Universal—for everybody, for king and slave, for black men as well as white,

This perplexed the heathen, and their rulers thought that Christ's Church was a secret political club which might become dangerous to the Government, and therefore must be suppressed.

But the chief reason why Christianity had to bear the full fury of the oppressor, was because the Church's voice gave no uncertain sound on the subject of idols: she declared boldly that "they be no gods which were made with hands," and that all who joined her must utterly renounce idols, and worship only the One True Living God.

So over and over again, the gigantic might of Rome, the mightiest nation, save our own, that the world has ever seen, was hurled against Christianity, but to no effect. The Church *cannot* fall, for it is the building of the Holy Spirit, and Christ is the Head Corner Stone.

Instead of being stamped out the Church spread more and more.

"The Blood of the Martyrs is the seed of the Church." Never was a truer saying. The more the enemy slew, and the fiercer the attack, the stronger and purer became the Church, and finally she herself conquered that proud Roman nation which had tried so hard to destroy her.

Trajan was one of the kindest of the Roman Emperors, yet he thought it his duty to be a bitter foe to Christianity.

He had occasion once, when he was on a visit to the East, to visit Antioch, where its inhabitants gave him a grand welcome, which included heathen practices that no Christian could join in, so they all kept away from the festivities.

Finding this out, Trajan summoned the aged Bishop of Antioch, as the head of them, to appear before him and be questioned about this failure in loyalty.

He was a wise and holy man, Ignatius by name, and had been a friend of the Apostle S. John. Some writers hold that he was actually the little child whom our Lord took and set in the midst of the disciples. The Emperor wanted to understand more about the Christian religion and asked, "Is it true, that you carry Him within you, who suffered under Pontius Pilate?"

With strong faith Ignatius replied: "Verily and indeed, for so it is written, 'I will dwell in them and walk in them.'"

Then said Trajan, "Thinkest thou not that we have the gods within us, who assist us in our battles against our enemies?"

"Thou dost err," Ignatius boldly replied. "There is but One God, and One Christ Jesus, the Only-Begotten Son of God, whose kingdom may I enjoy."

A few more questions followed, a few more

brave, courageous answers, and then came his doom. "Let Ignatius be carried to Rome and there be thrown to the wild beasts."

This time the Bishop's answer was a song of thanksgiving. "I thank Thee, O God, that Thou hast thought me worthy to glorify Thee by my death."

He was put in the charge of ten soldiers, who were to guard him safely throughout the long journey. How harsh and cruel they were to the gentle, aged Bishop we can read for ourselves in one of the many letters he wrote at that time.

He says, "From Syria even to Rome I fight with beasts by night and day, being bound to ten leopards, that is to say, a band of ten soldiers." Then he goes on, "I shall gladly suffer for Christ, I am His wheat, and ground by the teeth of wild beasts, shall be made the pure bread of Christ."

When his ship touched Ostia, there were still eighteen miles of road before he reached the Colosseum, the scene of his death struggle.

The weary Bishop was hurried along, for it was the last day of the heathen feast, and the spectacle of his agony was needed to amuse the populace.

When he reached the Amphitheatre, Ignatius was at once placed in the centre of the immense oval stage.

Silence was ordered to be kept, while the magistrate read out his death-warrant.

The people obeyed, but while the reading was proceeding, another noise that could not be silenced was distinctly heard—a noise like low underground thunder.

It was the noise of the starved and maddened lions, waiting to be let loose on the martyr.

The magistrate stopped—there was a breathless pause, then the keepers rolled back the strong iron gates of the dens, and two ferocious lions rushed on Ignatius.

His hour of triumph had come—one moment's sharp torture, and then,—the evermore rejoicing before his God.

Late that night three of the most daring of the Christians stole into the Colosseum, and, spreading out a cloth, they collected the blood-stained sand, and a few bones that the lions had left, and bore them away for reverent burial.

I have not the time to tell you, even a little, about the many martyrdoms—they were so numerous, so glorious. I can choose out just one or two, and some day perhaps you will read for yourselves the thrilling histories of those times.

You ought to know about S. Polycarp. He was appointed Bishop of Smyrna by S. John himself, and some believe him to be the "Angel" mentioned in the second chapter of the Book of the Revelation.

Our Lord Jesus there sends a message to the Christians in Smyrna, that they might be strengthened in the storm of persecution that was about to burst on them.

Perhaps nowhere was the storm more terrific; torture upon torture was heaped on them, but the Saviour's message rang in their ears: "Be thou faithful unto death," and obeying it they won the promised "Crown of Life."

The account of their sufferings can be read to-day in an epistle the poor survivors addressed to their brethren in the Churches of Pontus.

S. Polycarp, the Bishop, when seized and brought before his judge, was ordered to revile Christ, but answered,—

"Eighty and six years have I served Him, and He never forsook me; how can I now blaspheme my King?"

He was sentenced to be burnt alive. The pile was set alight, but the flames instead of scorching seemed to arch over him like the sail of a ship, and "he was in the midst, not like burning flesh, but as gold and silver purified in the fire." So wrote an eyewitness of the scene.

The persecutors, seeing his body could not be destroyed by fire, commanded an executioner to kill him with the sword, which was accordingly done.

In the Fifth Persecution, only a few years later,

the rich young Perpetua and her companions died heroically, while a slave at Alexandria, who was condemned to be lowered inch by inch into a cauldron of burning pitch, endured the agony for three hours, steadfastly confessing Christ the while, and by her marvellous devotion won over one of her torturers to the Christian Faith.

Many of the poor mangled bones of the martyrs found a resting-place in the Catacombs, that curious network of underground passages; here also in times of danger the Christians used to hide.

I myself have been in the Roman Catacombs. They consist of long, straight, narrow alleys, with shelves on each side, cut out of the wall, where the dead were laid.

Sometimes there is a larger opening into a kind of chapel, and this is generally sacred to the memory of a martyr whose tomb forms the altar.

These Catacombs have miles and miles of passages. No one knows how many; some say two hundred and fifty, some eight hundred! It is even reported that a few years back a schoolmaster took twenty of his boys to explore them, and they lost their way and have never been heard of since, though many search parties were sent out to rescue them.

If you want now to see the Catacombs you must take a guide, and every person has to carry a lighted candle. I took such care of mine, I was afraid of its going out and of being left behind in those dark burying-places.

Some of these Catacombs have five or six storeys, only instead of going *up* to the storeys, you go down deeper into the earth, by steep staircases.

When the persecutions became so fierce that Christians were searched for everywhere, they hid in the Catacombs, thinking they would be safer in those bewildering passages than in any other place.

It was useless leaving Rome, as they were liable to be caught and condemned throughout the country, so here the hunted Christians made their homes while the persecutions raged.

They blocked up the principal entrances which everyone knew about, and they made their way in by disused quarries and sandpits. They would climb down their steep sides as far as they dared, and then give a known signal. At this a friend would silently rear up a ladder from below, by which they descended. When the last person was safely down, the ladder was withdrawn and no trace of their having been there was left.

Christians, however, were not always safe in these dark cemeteries, even.

Once a party of soldiers discovered a number of believers, who probably had met together for worship, and all of them, men, women and children, were there and then walled up alive!

Another time, just after Sixtus, Bishop of Rome, had celebrated the Holy Communion and the congregation were ready to disperse, the dreaded sound of the tramp of soldiers' feet was heard. The Christians' hiding-place had been discovered! Sixtus was at once arrested and dragged away, followed by his weeping people.

At the entrance of the cemetery he was told to kneel. Then came a bright flash of steel—a heavy thud—and Sixtus passed from the Holy Communion on earth to the more Blessed Communion above.

Three days later, his chief deacon, Lawrence, one of the communicants on that solemn morning, was broiled alive on a huge gridiron, placed on the Viminal Hill at Rome.

You wonder how he can bear the agony! Listen! In the midst of it he is praying in clear low tones —for himself? No, like his dear Lord, he is praying for his tormentors, that they may become the people of God.

All is calm and holy about the martyr. Look at his face, radiant with joy!

He hardly seems to suffer, though gradually his voice grows fainter and fainter, and at length he gently falls asleep in his iron cradle.

No wonder that at sights like these the very heathen were amazed and talked about the patience and joyfulness of the Christians.

You might think that this Eighth Persecution, when these two Saints, amongst countless others, were slain, must have been the sorest. But it was surpassed perhaps in horror by the great Tenth Persecution in 303, the cruellest of all the onslaughts of the devil upon Christ's Church.

An Edict was published, stating that all Christians, of whatsoever rank, should be liable to torture: that churches which had been built during lulls in the persecutions should be razed to the ground: that all meetings for prayer and the Sacraments should cease, and that the Scriptures and other Service-books should be burned. Judges were ordered to find new ways of tormenting the Christians.

Imagine the consternation and dismay in the Church when they knew of this proclamation.

Do you think they kept away from worship, or from partaking of the Holy Communion on account of it?

No, they dared disobey an earthly monarch, but not the King of Kings, and Lord of Lords. Besides, their one comfort was in drawing near to their Saviour in those dark days: strengthened by His Body and Blood they felt they could face any pain.

They had, however, to turn the most wonderful places into churches for the time being: sometimes a gloomy cave in the side of a mountain, or even a large hollow tree. Once they chose the middle of a swamp, where at every step they sank knee-deep in the black mire, and they had to be carefully guided by a Christian who knew the spot well, for deep pits abounded, which in a moment would completely swallow up the unsuspecting traveller.

But then all these dangers diminished the risk of discovery by their enemies, and so were cheerfully faced.

Now what I want you never to forget is that our Church is the very same as the Church to which these early Christians belonged. Even nowadays, in distant parts of the world, the same sort of persecution often attacks the Church of Jesus Christ.

Think what noble martyrs only recently witnessed for their Saviour in China — women and little children as well as men, bearing torture as awful as these you have been reading about.

Have you been told, too, about those black boys in Uganda who became Christians and refused to give up their religion for all the threats of their savage chief?

He ordered them to have their arms cut off, and then to be slowly roasted alive. This was in January 1885.

God's Holy Spirit strengthened them to bear the pain and even to sing through it.

We know the very words they sang—a verse of that beautiful hymn,—

"Daily, daily sing to Jesus,
Sing my soul His praises due;
All He does deserves our praises,
And our deep devotion too.
For in deep humiliation,
He for us did live below,
Died on Calvary's Cross of torture,
Rose to save our souls from woe."

They sang till no more sound could pass those poor dried-up lips—but when that faint song on earth was finished, they joined the glorious choir of the redeemed on high.

Surely these were martyrs as noble as S. Lawrence, though one died in the third, and the other in the nineteenth century.

Coming to our own land, I have read, in a book of anecdotes by the Rev. A. G. Jackson, about an English workman in one of our big potteries who would not join in the swearing and gambling that went on about him. His companions were rough, bad men, who felt irritated because he stood aloof from their wickedness, and he seemed to them like a perpetual reproach.

One day the devil prompted them to a terrible plan. They seized "the saint" as they named him, and forced him to stand before the awful heat of a furnace, vowing they would keep him there till he should swear blasphemous oaths like the rest of them.

The heat was terrible, agonizing, but he never opened his mouth; they kept him longer and longer in torture, till the men themselves got frightened for fear their brutality should be discovered and punished, and they released the sufferer.

His clergyman got to hear of his being on the sick list, and the cause of it, and he questioned the man on the matter.

"What did you think about, John, when you stood before that scorching furnace?"

He quietly answered, "I can't rightly tell, sir. I only know I never before felt the Lord so near me."

Through all the centuries there is the same Loving Presence, the same help, the same faith, the same joy in suffering and the same welcome on high for those who confess Christ before men.

"All that will live godly in Christ Jesus shall suffer persecution," the Bible tells us.

We may be spared the extreme tortures the martyrs had to endure, but suffering in some shape will come if we are true to our Lord.

It may be abuse when we refuse to join in

some wrong-doing, or, more trying still, the mocking laugh when we show Whose we are and Whom we serve.

These seem trifles, but they are hard to bear, and no one knows that better than the tender Saviour, who, if we will only try to do the right, will strengthen us to be victors and will reward us with a wondrous joy that no earthly pleasure or advantage ever gives.

"If we suffer, we shall also reign with Him."

CHAPTER III

Glastonbury Abbey—Romans Conquer Britain—The Thundering Legion—S. Alban

"The people which sat in darkness saw great Light."

WE long to know who were the first messengers who brought the faith of Jesus to our land, but no one can tell us with certainty.

Very brave and devoted they must have been, for terrible tales were told about the barbarous tribes that used to live in Britain. They were said to be cannibals, and S. Jerome, a famous Christian writer who lived about 400 years after the birth of our Lord, mentions that he himself saw in the Roman army a body of savage soldiers, who came from the north of our island, and were said to be fed on human flesh. Although in this he was doubtless misinformed, we know how powerful and cruel was the false religion of the Druids, whose headquarters were in Anglesey, a religion that continually caused the sacrifice of human victims.

Oh, what a wonderful breaking in of light upon their darkness must the good news brought by the Church have been to the followers of this ghastly superstition.

No longer now need their loved ones be snatched from them to be tortured and slain, for they learnt that the Saviour had come, who had Himself made "a full, perfect, and sufficient sacrifice for the sins of the whole world."

Some think that S. Paul first told the "good-spell" to Britain, and five years of his life are certainly unaccounted for between his examination and release by Nero and his second trial and condemnation in 68. Clement, whom you will find named in the epistle to the Philippians, says that S. Paul preached the Gospel to "the uttermost bounds of the West." America was not known then, nor till fourteen centuries later, so this expression clearly meant that S. Paul reached Spain on his missionary journeys. Possibly, it included Britain, though there is no proof, or even strong tradition, that S. Paul actually came to our shores. So we must not feel at all sure about it, much as we should like to think that one of our Lord's Apostles had really been here.

Others say that S. Joseph of Arimathea with twelve companions came to a little island in Somerset named Avalon. It was winter-time when they arrived, but the legend is that after S. Joseph had planted his staff in the ground it blossomed into lovely flowers; from this he concluded that he was meant to stop there, and bring to God the sweet flowers of souls converted from heathenism.

The Holy Thorn, as it got to be called, was considered a miracle, and much money came to Avalon and Bristol by selling cuttings from this celebrated tree to foreign countries.

That was the age when even the most natural things were looked upon as miracles. It is well known to botanists that there is a species of thorn that blossoms twice a year; but I am sure it must be rare, or people would not for many ages have considered this one such a wonder.

It is only a legend that S. Joseph of Arimathea came to Glastonbury, as the spot is now called. But some Christian teacher did certainly come there in very early times, and build a church of mud and wattle, or basket work; and there are still twelve portions of land, called the twelve hidæ, of which no one knows the original owners. Eight hundred years ago the Doomsday Book was written by William the Conqueror's orders. It was an inventory or list of all the houses and lands in England, and there it is stated that "these twelve hidæ never have been taxed," showing that for long ages before the Conquest they were Church property.

Avalon, or Glastonbury, was considered a very sacred spot. Kings and great men paid large sums to be buried there, King Arthur of the Round Table being the most celebrated of them all.

As time rolled on a stately abbey was built on the site of the wattle church. Henry VIII. coveted its treasures and hanged Whiting, the last Abbot, on the hill above the town; a good, generous-hearted old man of eighty, whose sole offence was that he would not tamely surrender the church and its property to that sacrilegious King.

This earliest Christian monastery in Britain is now only a beautiful ruin. The Holy Thorn is cut down, but we need not mourn over that, for the villagers had grown plants of it in their gardens, and every May and December these put forth the same lovely blossoms that are said to have so cheered the heart of S. Joseph of Arimathea.

Other names have been suggested as the first missionaries to our Island, but now it is most generally thought that the Gospel was brought to us by Christian soldiers in the Roman armies who were sent here.

Tertullian, the Latin historian, writing in 208, mentions that "in districts of Britain unaccessible to the Roman, but subdued to Christ, in all these the Kingdom and Name of Christ are venerated."

A century later we had a fully-organised Church,

with Bishops, Priests, and Deacons; for at a Council, held in 314, at Arles in France, the British Church sent representatives of the three orders of Ministry.

We know even the names of those who went. Perhaps you would like to hear them, they are so different from names in the present day.

Eborius, . . .	Bishop of York.
Restitutus, . . .	Bishop of London.
Adelfius, . . .	Bishop of Lincoln.
* * * . . .	Priest.
Arminius, . . .	Deacon.

You know the reason of the presence of a Roman army in Britain? Twice under Julius Cæsar they had invaded our shores, and 100 years later the southern portion of England was completely conquered by them.

Not without hard fighting, though; for the British were a formidable foe, especially when they dashed with their war chariots, which had scythes fastened to the wheels, into the midst of the enemy's ranks, mowing down the soldiers like corn; or when they checked the foreign army's advance through their woods by fastening branches of trees together into a sort of strong basket work, which had to be hewn down before any progress could be made.

But all their efforts to save their country were

powerless before the great civilized nation that had come against them, though they did succeed in keeping Ireland and the North of Scotland unconquered.

But, indeed, the coming of the Romans was really a great blessing to the land.

They drained the marshes, and cut down the tangled forests, turning them into pastures and cornfields. They also made magnificent roads, which remain to this day.

Right through their vast dominions these roads were cut and paved and kept in splendid repair. Every few miles were posting-houses where horses could be changed, and by doing so frequently, a journey of 150 miles could be made in one day. So perfect was the Roman system of communication by sea and land, that it was possible to go over 4000 miles, through different countries, without any hindrance.

Thus unknowingly, and thinking only of making their own Empire secure, the Romans had been used by God to prepare a way by which Christ's message could be proclaimed throughout the world. Two legions of the Roman army were generally stationed in Britain, and sometimes three.

That Christianity had taken deep root among the soldiers need not surprise us when we remember that both S. Paul and S. Peter were in captivity in Rome and for some time were actually chained to Roman soldiers; and you may be sure this opportunity of teaching their keepers the true Faith would be made the most of by the Apostles.

There is a beautiful story of the "Thundering Legion" which I will tell you, as it shows how Christianity had spread among the army. Some people think it is only a legend, but we actually find confirmation of it from the heathens themselves in a sculpture which is still to be seen on the column raised to the memory of the Emperor Aurelius.

This Emperor in the hottest part of the summer of 174 was carrying on war with a savage tribe called the Quadi, a very trying foe as they never would engage in a pitched battle, but retreated directly the Romans got near them; something like what the Boers have done in our South African war.

The hot weather, their heavy armour, but above all the scarcity of water, indeed they were suffering from water famine, had thoroughly disheartened the soldiers. Had it been possible, Aurelius would have led the army back, but over two long days' march lay between their present position and the last stream they had seen. Ere they could reach it scarce a man would have been alive to drink the precious water; and yet how could they advance with that awful craving on them?

All seemed hopeless, and, to make matters worse, the enemy suddenly appeared in the distance, evidently counting on an easy victory over the distressed soldiers.

It was a desperate case. Defeat and death seemed close upon the Romans, look what way they would. Prayers had been offered to the heathen god of battles and the god of rain, but to no avail.

"Call upon Me in the time of trouble," says our Almighty Father, and the Christians in that Legion remembered this, and asked permission to unite in prayer to Him who sitteth above the water-floods.

All other means having failed, the heathen Emperor gave them leave to try their plan.

The Christian soldiers knelt to pray under a deep blue sky, with a burning sun beating down on them, but as they rose from their knees a slight breeze had sprung up, driving a grey cloud or two before it.

Soon a rolling bank of darkness hid the sun, and the first drops of that long-desired shower fell!

The men tore off their helmets in their frantic earnestness to lose none of the refreshing water; but there was no fear of scarcity, faster and faster fell the rain, till man and beast had enough and to spare.

Meanwhile the Quadi drew nearer, and then, as the battle was about to begin, such a thunder-storm burst, that the barbarians fled in terror and confusion.

The Romans were victorious! The greater number of these, who were heathen, said that the storm came through the magical arts of a celebrated magician who accompanied the army, but the Christian soldiers knew that their Saviour's words had once again been found faithful. "Whatsoever ye shall ask the Father in My Name He will give it you."

As a rule our island escaped those great persecutions that fell on the Christians in other parts. The names of two martyrs have, however, been handed down to us, Aaron and Julius, but we know nothing certain about their martyrdom, though some name Chester as the place where it occurred.

With a third, S. Alban, it is different. Our own Church historian, the Venerable Bede, has told us all about him.

He was a rich young Roman noble, living in his own villa at Verulam, kind and generous by nature, and ever ready to protect the weak.

One day a Christian priest named Amphibalus sought shelter under his roof from persecution. This was readily granted, and the priest remained hidden many days in that luxurious house.

Alban had been educated at Rome and therefore must have heard something about the Christian religion: he narrowly observed his visitor, and was struck by his reverence at prayer and by the holiness of his life.

Always remember our manner of living is a far more striking sermon than our words.

He began to question Amphibalus about his Creed. How happy must the priest have then been. His hiding-hole became a glorious church wherein he could preach Christ Crucified.

Day after day Alban came to hear more about his Saviour. He knew well that if he became a Christian, he, too, most likely, would be persecuted and have to give up his riches and his beautiful home and perhaps even lay down life itself.

But then, on the other hand, he learned that all who became Christians by baptism, and so joined the Church, had far better things given them than these earthly treasures.

They had the knowledge that God was with them wherever they were: no matter what the danger, "underneath are the Everlasting Arms." No matter what the torture or death, Jesus was standing waiting to receive them. White robes, the crown of glory, the new song of the redeemed, perpetual joy were theirs in that happy land where God dwells.

As Alban listened, he saw the perishing things of earth in their true light, dim and uncertain, and knew that the lasting things of Heaven alone were worth caring for, and he declared that he would be a Christian unto death.

He was baptized, and then Amphibalus wished to move further on, to win other souls for Christ, but his newly-baptized son entreated him to stay a little longer to help him on the heavenly path.

The priest consented, but Alban and he had only a few days of talk and counsel together. Somehow the secret leaked out that Amphibalus was hiding in the young noble's villa, and suddenly a guard of soldiers surrounded the house.

In that moment of alarm Alban was collected and unselfish. He insisted on changing cloaks with the priest, so allowing Amphibalus to escape undetected.

Alban himself was seized, the soldiers naturally thinking at first that they had really caught the priest. Even when the mistake was discovered, the judge declared that unless he sacrificed to the heathen gods, all the punishment due to the priest should fall on his head.

He boldly refused with the words, "I worship the One True, Living God, who created all things.'

He was thereupon cruelly tortured and sentenced to be beheaded on the hill at the other side of the stream.

The news of the capture and condemnation of so rich and popular an inhabitant spread like wildfire through the town, and the whole population came out to witness the martyrdom.

The narrow bridge spanning the river became densely packed with the excited crowd, but so full of hope and joy was Alban, so anxious not to be delayed in witnessing for his Lord, that he would not wait for the bridge to be cleared, but dashed through the water to the place of execution.

One soldier who was told off to give the fatal stroke put down his sword, refusing the task, and declaring himself a Christian. Both were beheaded at the same time.

We do not know the soldier's name, but a glorious cathedral marks the site of the joint martyrdom and bears the name of the Roman noble, while since those days the town itself has ceased to be called Verulam and is known only by the name of S. Albans.

A short time after this, Amphibalus was captured and put to a painful death, and we doubt not that he too was ready and glad to "be with Christ, which is far better."

Soon after this, persecution ceased and Christianity became the religion of the Romans and of Romanized Britain, though Ireland and parts of Scotland were still in heathen darkness.

Churches, of course, were now being built in Britain. The oldest church that remains to this day, and perhaps the oldest Christian building in the world, is S. Mary le Castle at Dover. Though it has stood for 1600 years, it still looks strong enough to last for many generations to come.

S. Martin's at Canterbury is, I believe, nearly as ancient. Queen Bertha found it ready built when she came over from France to be King Ethelbert's wife, and she used it as her private chapel more than 1300 years ago.

The rest of the Church buildings were destroyed in the terrible devastation caused by the heathen Jutes, Angles, and Saxons, when they conquered our land, as you will read in the next chapter.

CHAPTER IV

Fall of Rome—Picts and Scots harass the Britons—S. Germanus and the Hallelujah Battle—The Saxons —Lives of S. Patrick and S. Columba

"The Isles shall wait upon Me."

THE Roman Empire was falling to pieces through its own corruption and wickedness.

In 410 the crash came, when Rome herself, the proud city that had ruled for twelve centuries, was overrun and sacked by her barbarian conquerors.

For some time past all her soldiers had been recalled from the colonies, to save the mother country.

Every fighting man, were he Roman or Briton, was taken from our island; for British warriors were greatly valued on account of their bravery and strength.

Now came the opportunity for the Picts and Scots, fierce tribes inhabiting Scotland, to attack the defenceless Britons, their ancient enemies.

The Romans had tried to shut them out by

building a great stone wall, 8 feet broad, 12 feet high and 68 miles long, right across the country from the mouth of the Tyne to the Solway Firth. This was now only manned by trembling lads, and old men, who "pined away day and night in the utmost fear."

"On the other side the enemy attacked them with hooked weapons by which the cowardly defenders were dragged from the wall and dashed against the ground. At last the Britons, forsaking their cities and wall, took to flight and were dispersed. The enemy pursued, and the slaughter was greater than on any former occasion, for the wretched natives were torn in pieces by their enemies, as lambs are torn by wild beasts."

Just as that time of blood-shedding, S. Ninian, a missionary, ventured to come to these very fierce savages. We know very little about him except that he built a church of white stone, and dedicated it to his friend S. Martin, of whose death he had recently heard. So different was this church in construction from the mud and wattle huts of the Picts that they called it the White House, and Whithorn the town is named to this very day. It is situated in Wigtownshire, and if ever you go there you must visit S. Ninian's cave, where many ancient Christian treasures have been discovered lately.

Ninian must have been getting old when Palladius, another missionary, came to help in converting the Picts, and he built a church at Fordun. He had been first sent to Ireland "to strengthen the Scotii believing in Christ," but he had failed in this mission.

I must here explain that, in these early times, Scots always meant people living in Ireland!

After a time the Scots crossed over the narrowest channel of the sea and settled in Britain. By-and-by so many came and conquered the land of the Picts, that at length Scot-land became the name of that part of the country, and has remained so ever since, while all the people in Ireland were called Irish.

Terrible days those were for the British, both within and without the Church.

Within the Church, a Welshman named Pelagius had begun to teach mistaken doctrines. He said man had no need of the grace of God to help him to do right, but that he could of his own self keep from sinning. This was grievously wrong, and the error had poisoned the minds of the British Christians.

Some people think that it does not matter what you believe if you "lead a good life," as they say. This is a very serious mistake. God has given us His holy Word that we may believe rightly, and has founded His Church to guard and explain His Word and His Will; surely, therefore, it is very wrong not to believe what God has taught us.

The British Church became alarmed at the spread of this false teaching, and in 429 sent for help from Gaul, as France was then called. The good Bishop Germanus with a friend came over at once, to try and bring back the Christians to the true faith.

They went about the country preaching and teaching the people what they ought to believe. Crowds flocked to hear them and obeyed their instructions, so that Britain was saved from this heresy.

Once, when they were in Flintshire and had just baptized a large number of heathen Britons, news was brought that those dreaded enemies the Picts were swooping down on them.

S. Germanus, who had been a soldier before he became a Bishop, told his converts, as they gathered round him in their white baptismal robes, that, unarmed as they were, they need not be afraid of the enemy. He bade them stand in ranks, surrounded by their watch fires, and when the Picts appeared they were to sing together with all their might a hymn of triumph that he had just taught them.

They were in a little valley surrounded by rocky

hills, with a river running through it. S. Germanus held the standard, and, at the first sight of the dreaded enemy, he gave the signal for the song of praise.

In an instant a burst louder than of thunder alarmed their foes. "Hallelujah, Hallelujah, Hallelujah!" The hills re-echoed the word, and the astonished Picts were seized with panic, "fearing that not only the neighbouring rocks, but even the skies were falling on them." They fled precipitately, casting away their weapons to run the quicker from such mysterious sights and sounds. Many were drowned in the river Mold, while the Britons won the "Hallelujah Battle" without the loss of a man. The name of the field where the armies met is still called "Maes Garmon," or the Field of Germanus.

For the time the heresy of Pelagius was stamped out, and the Bishops returned to Gaul.

A few years later it showed itself again, and once more Germanus visited Britain to root it up, this time he was thoroughly successful.

Thus the inward trouble of the Church was removed, but the trouble from without grew more and more terrible.

In an evil day, the poor Britons, worn out with trying to keep back their fierce enemies the Picts and Scots, invited the powerful Saxons, a German tribe, to come and help them in their fighting, promising rewards for their services.

The Saxons came over in swarms and defeated the enemies of the British, but instead of going back again when their work was over, they thought our country looked a nice land for them to settle in, so they seized farms, villages, and even towns, butchering the inhabitants to make room for themselves.

I daresay many of you have been on an excursion to Eastbourne and have rambled over Pevensey Castle. It used to be called Andredscester, and we know exactly what happened there when the Saxons besieged and took it, for the account is written in their Anglo-Saxon Chronicle.

This is the entry:—

"491. This year Ella and Cissa besieged Andredscester, and slew all that dwelt therein, so that not a single Briton was there left."

This shows their style of warfare—no wonder that Christianity was soon extinct wherever they conquered. They especially hated priests and churches; and at last the only place of safety for the poor Britons was the very west of their island.

Here they were left fairly undisturbed, and hither the Bishops of London and York with their clergy fled for fear of the Saxon sword.

In their mountain fastnesses the persecuted Church still lifted up her daily voice of prayer and praise, while the rest of their beloved country was once again plunged into the darkness of heathenism.

Some have blamed the British for not trying to convert their conquerors, but it is most unlikely that these would have deigned to listen to the race they had subdued and enslaved. Then, too, if our parents had been murdered and our property seized, should we have been very ready to come forward and teach our cruel oppressors the way heavenward? It would require great grace from God to do it.

Just at this time when Christianity was being swept out of a great part of Britain by heathen invaders, it was spreading with marvellous rapidity in Ireland.

The apostle of the Irish was S. Patrick, a Briton who lived close to the Roman wall. His father was a deacon, and his grandfather a priest, so that his childhood had been passed in a Christian home. Not that he thought much of that great blessing at the time, even as we often forget to thank God for the love and Christianity that surrounds us. When trouble, however, came on Patrick he was able to turn to that God of his fathers and find Him indeed an ever-present help.

The Scots, who, as I told you, came from Ireland, chanced one day, on one of their frequent plundering expeditions, to visit the farm where Patrick's parents lived. They carried off Patrick, then a lad of sixteen, and his two sisters, to sell them as slaves in Ireland.

Patrick became the property of Milchu, King of North Dalaradia, a harsh master, by whom he was sent to be a shepherd on the mountains—a lonely and miserable life for a lad who had been brought up in a happy home. Sometimes he was drenched by rain, sometimes frozen with cold. For six years this was his lot, hard years of bondage, but in them God was preparing him for the great work he was afterwards to do.

Left alone with God, Patrick learnt to know and trust Him as he never could have done otherwise. In after-life the most terrible dangers (and he was in many) never made him quail: he knew for a certainty that he was perfectly safe in his heavenly Father's keeping, whatever might happen.

When he was twenty-two years of age he managed to escape and return safely to his family. What a meeting that must have been; no wonder his parents said that they never could let him leave them again.

Patrick, however, withstood their entreaties. He felt he had had a divine call to preach to the heathen people of Ireland, and he dared not disregard it.

In those days the only schools, or colleges, were the monasteries, where the clergy lived together under a common rule; and S. Patrick determined to study at them, and so prepare himself for being a missionary.

First he went to the monastery of S. Martin of Tours in France, where the famous founder, Martin, the soldier-Bishop, had died not long before. Then he passed on to the school of Germanus of Auxerre, where he probably arrived just before S. Germanus came over to strengthen the faith of the Britons.

Afterwards S. Patrick went to Lérins, which was one of the most famous of all the schools of learning at that time.

Lérins consists of two islands close together. The one which had the monastery on it was called S. Honorat, as that was the founder's name. It is a lovely little island of white rock rising out of the deep blue Mediterranean Sea, with pine trees fringing the waters, and right round the island are remains of many very tiny churches.

The monastery is once more used as a college, and I have seen the students dressed like little monks walking about; but I have not been able to go over the monastery, as women are only allowed inside the gates one day in the year, and I was not fortunate enough ever to be there on that occasion.

When S. Patrick had received sufficient book-learning, he went back to Auxerre to be ordained deacon, and, after working hard in that capacity, he was made a priest and then consecrated as Bishop of the Irish.

Whom do you think he earnestly wished to bring first to the feet of Jesus? Why, the very cross old king whose slave he had been for six years. Remembering, however, that he had run away from him without giving any compensation, he brought in his hand the sum of money which Milchu had originally paid to possess him, for he knew that it was written in God's Word, "Owe no man anything." The old king was unsoftened by Patrick's honesty. He was furious at a slave presuming to teach him, and he refused to have anything to do with S. Patrick, or his new religion. This must have been a very great disappointment, but Patrick let nothing weigh him down. The cause was God's, and in the end it must succeed.

The first convert he baptized was Dichu, also a king; from his home S. Patrick went to preach round and "the Faith began to spread."

After a time he took longer journeys and reached Tara, the chief town of a very powerful heathen king, who encouraged and surrounded himself with magicians. S. Patrick was in the utmost danger there and he knew it.

He composed a hymn, which is really a prayer in poetry, that God would preserve him in this time of peril. It is very long, but so beautiful that I must copy out a few lines for you. This is a translation published by the S.P.C.K., as the original is written in a very ancient Irish dialect.

> "Christ, as a Light
> Illumine and guide me!
> Christ, as a shield, o'ershadow and cover me!
> Christ be under me, Christ be over me,
> Christ be beside me
> On left hand and right!
> Christ be before me, behind me, about me!
> Christ, this day, be within and without me!
>
> Christ, the lowly and meek,
> Christ, the all-powerful, be
> In the heart of each to whom I speak,
> In the heart of each who speaks to me,
> In all who draw near me
> Or see me, or hear me!"

An old author writes "it is held in great esteem by the Irish ever since, for it is believed and proved by long experience to preserve from imminent dangers, both of soul and body, those who devoutly recite it." We need not smile at this, or doubt its truth, for our God is a "God that heareth prayer," and this hymn is a true prayer for protection. I have read that to this present day the Irish peasantry use this hymn at their evening prayers.

Later on S. Patrick founded Armagh, whose Bishop became Metropolitan, or Archbishop, over all Ireland; but its beginning was very humble, a few buildings made of osier, moss and mud, and sometimes a grander one of wood. First to be constructed in those days of perpetual warfare was always a fort or protecting fence, then the church, the clergy hut, and the kitchen, which most likely was dining-room too. Of course as Christians multiplied these would be enlarged and improved.

Directly S. Patrick had gathered a Christian community, however small, he would ordain and consecrate the three orders of Ministry, as our Lord commanded, Bishop, Priest, and Deacon, that they might guard the flock and keep up unceasingly the work and services of the Church. Then S. Patrick would go forth to break up fresh ground, and wage the heavenly war, cheered and strengthened by the thought of the many prayers that were ascending to the throne of God from the centres of Christianity that he had already established.

His plan was to gain the chief, or king, first, and then the tribe would be more likely to follow.

One part of his work was most dangerous—the

throwing down of heathen idols. The magicians and common people were enraged at this. The biggest idol in all Ireland was King Laoghaire's, and was thought to be most sacred. It was a huge "black stooping-stone" in the middle of a plain surrounded by twelve other idols of brass. The whole of them were felled by S. Patrick, which so exasperated a chieftain of Leinster that he vowed he would not rest till he had taken the Saint's life.

But Oran, his charioteer, got to hear of these threats, and expected that the attempt would be made while they were passing through the chief's domains on a preaching tour. As they got near his castle, therefore, Oran pretended to feel ill, and asked S. Patrick if he would mind walking a little, and let him ride in the chariot till he was better. S. Patrick consented at once, never dreaming of his servant's noble self-sacrifice.

They were now close underneath the fort, and there hiding in some bushes near to the path was the fanatic chieftain with a javelin in his hand.

He heard the chariot approaching, and, with unerring aim, threw his weapon right at the heart of its occupant, and mortally wounded, not S. Patrick, as he hoped, but the faithful servant Oran.

S. Patrick himself died peacefully at a good old

age, close to the church that King Dichu, his first convert, had helped him to build. Full of joy and thankfulness must he have been at the success of his mission. No wonder that the Irish love to call their children by his name, and that so many little "Pats" are running about in Ireland now.

S. Patrick had a grand helper in the conversion of the Irish in S. Bridget, the founder of many religious houses. Numerous churches have been named in memory of her, S. Bridget or S. Bride.

The great heart of S. Patrick had not been content with having Ireland as a field of work. Across the waters he sent S. Piran to Cornwall, whose original church was only a few years ago accidentally discovered buried in the sand. When first dug out it was in good preservation, but when I saw it in 1900 it had greatly crumbled away with exposure to the air. Learned people who have examined the tiny building say that it must have been erected about the year 500. S. Piran lies buried there.

Missionaries from Ireland went as far north as the Faroe Islands and Iceland, and all over the continent of Europe. No one of them, however, was more famous than S. Columba.

He was born of royal parents a few years after S. Patrick's death, and in 563, after he had founded several monasteries in Ireland, he set out in the full strength of his perfect manhood to work for Christ among the savage Picts.

Many reasons are given for his going. Some say it was "for love of souls," and that we may be sure it was, whatever other causes may have had a part in the decision.

Another account is that he went as a penance. It seems that Columba greatly admired a certain Psalter that belonged to one Finnian, and copied it secretly in the church at nights without asking permission to do so. Finnian found out what was going on, and claimed the copy as his property as it had been made from his book.

Columba, naturally enough, did not agree to this, so Finnian applied to the king for advice; you will like to hear his answer,—

"To every cow belongs its calf."

This, of course, meant that Columba was to give his copy to Finnian. He was very angry, and excited his tribe to rebellion, and a battle was fought in which Columba's side won, but not without heavy slaughter.

A Council of the Church was then held, in which Columba was condemned for having caused bloodshed. His sentence was that he must leave Ireland and win as many souls for Christ as the bodies that through his wrath had been slain in battle.

That famous Psalter can still be seen in the

library of the Royal Irish Academy, and it has ever since been called "The Book of Battle."

Columba, with twelve friends, set out in their skin-covered wicker boat, and at length landed on a little island near the Scotch coast, about 3 miles long and 1½ broad, called Iona.

Here they began at once to build a monastery; I suppose it was at first very like the one S. Patrick built at Armagh, or those he had himself built in Ireland; he little thought how world-famous Iona was to become.

Here the Kings of Scotland were crowned for a long period. The stone on which they sat for their coronation was a very sacred one, and had been brought from Ireland, where it had been venerated from remote antiquity. Indeed, the tradition is that it was the very stone that Jacob had for a pillow at Bethel when he fled from Esau, as you read in Genesis xxviii. 18. It rests now under the Coronation Chair of our Sovereigns in Westminster Abbey.

Columba was tall and strong, of kingly bearing and talents, and had a voice that could be heard at a great distance. There were few things that he could not do. He was a good sailor, artist, carpenter, miller, farmer, preacher, ruler, teacher, priest! No wonder, then, that men flocked to his monastery and willingly obeyed him.

His rule, though, was very strict. "Obedience unto Death" was commanded. Not even a shoe-lace could his followers claim as their own. During the fast of Lent the first food they tasted was after sunset. At other times two meals a day were allowed, dinner at noon, and supper.

There was no lack of work at Iona: farming, the plough being dragged by hand! fishing, schooling, teaching, sewing, for the monks had to make all their own clothes: besides which they went to church about three times a day. Columba's monks were expected to know the Psalter or the whole Book of Psalms off by heart, and they also learnt Latin and Greek. Moreover, all books that were used in the monastery were written out by the monks themselves.

For two years Columba stopped on or near the Island of Iona, to set all in working order, and then he left on an important missionary expedition to stern King Brude of the Northern Picts. After three years spent in Christianizing his subjects, he passed on to the Southern Picts.

When too old to travel, he devoted himself to prayer and study and to copying out God's Word.

On his last day of earthly life he was busy writing out the 34th Psalm, but he stopped suddenly after finishing the verse—"They who seek the Lord shall want no manner of thing that is good." He put down his pen remarking, "The next words belong rather to my successor Baithen, than to me." These were the words: "Come, ye children, and hearken unto me, and I will teach you the fear of the Lord."

He went to vespers, or evening prayer, and then lay down on his stone couch, till at midnight the monastery bell rang for matins.

Without waiting for a lantern, he groped his way into the church, and knelt before the altar. There the brethren coming in with their lights a minute or two later found him, and knew by his looks that the Master's Call, "Come up higher," had been heard.

They broke out into deep lamentations; he tried to raise his right hand and pronounce the Blessing, but nerve and voice failed, and with a smile on his face "he fell asleep."

This was on Whitsunday 597, a day of many memories besides that of the death of S. Columba.

CHAPTER V

S. Gregory and English Slaves—S. Augustine sent to England—British Church remains independent—S. Paulinus

"The heathen shall fear Thy Name, O Lord."

THE Saxons, and the Jutes, and Angles, who joined with them in invading England, had not long settled down in the lands they had wrenched from the British, when they began to quarrel among themselves.

They fought battles with each other, and the captives they took in war they sold as slaves to different countries. Rome needed many slaves just then, so it happened about the year 585 that English boys were being sold in her slave market.

The lads were young nobles or princes, as they wore their hair long as a sign of high rank; it hung down in golden curls, and made them look very different, with their blue eyes and fair skins, to the dark Southerners who surrounded them.

A Roman deacon named Gregory was struck by the beauty of the fresh faces and asked where they came from. On being told that their country was Britain, he further questioned the slave-dealers:—

"Are the islanders Christian or heathen?" On hearing they were pagan, he sighed deeply, saying, "Alas that such *fair* faces should be subjects of the Prince of *dark*ness; such *grace*ful bodies should not possess the *grace* of God in their souls!"

He wanted to know more still about these lads, and well for us he did, as you will see.

"What are their people called?" he asked.

"Angles," was the reply.

"Well named," exclaimed Gregory, "for they have the faces of Angels and are meet to be fellow-heirs with the Angels in Heaven."

"What name has their King?" he went on.

"Alle."

"Allelujah—for their land shall sing the praise of God their Maker;" and Gregory meant to act on these words. He went off at once to the Pope, that is, the Bishop of Rome, and asked to be sent as a missionary to Britain. He gave him permission, but told him to say nothing about his journey, as he was so beloved by the people that they might try and prevent his starting. No wonder they loved him, for his whole aim in life was to walk in the Saviour's footsteps, and, like Him, to go about "doing good."

The large marble table where he fed twelve hungry men daily may still be seen. He turned his own villa into a monastery, and his money, for he was rich, was spent in helping the poor, and in setting slaves free. Rome was full of trouble in those days, and its citizens rightly looked on Gregory as their best friend.

He therefore left Rome secretly, but his absence was soon discovered, and then what an outcry was made!

The people would not be content until mounted messengers had been sent after Gregory to bring him back to them again.

Thus for the time he was baffled in his plan, but he never forgot the handsome English lads, and their sad state of ignorance about God. He had a great friend, too, Eulogius, Patriarch or Bishop of Alexandria, who was very earnest about foreign missions, and especially anxious that Gregory should convert our island, and he wrote many letters to him on the subject.

At last Gregory's opportunity came: he was made Pope, or Bishop, and though he could not go himself, he was able to send a large party of missionaries to the work. At the head of them was Augustine, the Abbot of Gregory's own monastery, and with him were about forty priests and singers.

Alas! they were a timid set of men, and when they had gone a little way, and heard tales about the barbarous people among whom they were to live, they sent Augustine back to Rome to tell Pope Gregory that they were frightened, and to ask his leave to abandon the mission.

Terribly grieved must Gregory have been at their half-heartedness. How he must have longed once more to take the work in hand himself, but he knew this was impossible, so he strengthened his brethren. He wrote a kind, but very firm, letter, and told Augustine to return to the party with it.

This is how it began :—

"Gregory, the servant of the servants of God, to the servants of our Lord.

"Forasmuch as it had been better not to begin a good work, than to think of desisting from that which has been begun, it behoves you, my beloved sons, to fulfil the good work of the Lord you have undertaken. Let not therefore the toil of the journey, nor the tongues of evil-speaking men deter you. Almighty God protect you with His grace."

The missionaries need not have been so frightened. The Saxons, it is true, were heathen, but they were ripe for conversion to Christianity. Their King, Ethelbert, had himself married a

Christian princess, Bertha, daughter of the King of Paris, and she had been allowed to bring with her into Kent, Bishop Luidhart as her chaplain. The old British Church of S. Martin in Canterbury was given to them, and was thus once more hallowed by Holy Sacraments and prayers.

Over and over again had this little band of believers sent across the sea to Gaul for help to convert the heathen around them, but no one came. There was then no kind S. Germanus, who the century before had come directly he was told of the need to preach the Faith. S. Augustine therefore ought to have felt sure of Queen Bertha's welcome and prayers in the centre of his sphere of work. There was everything to encourage rather than discourage, but this Italian mission lacked the burning earnestness of the Irish or Celtic Apostles, whom no dangers daunted.

Nevertheless, these monks, though timid, were good, earnest men; and it was a great blessing to our island that they did come, for to begin with, they linked us to the grand organization and civilization of the Western Church, the Church of Rome.

You must understand clearly that the Church of Rome at that time was very different from the Church of Rome nowadays.

Like the Church of England, she is still a branch

of Christ's Holy Catholic Church, with her Bishops, Priests, and Deacons, descended like ours in succession from the Apostles, but she is a branch with a blight on it, the blight of error.

I will give you one instance to show you how differently she acts now to what she did in Pope Gregory's time.

Now, the Roman Church insists that divine worship shall everywhere be conducted exactly as she has it in Rome, and no other way. But Gregory the Great told Augustine to "choose from *every* Church, those things that are pious, religious, and upright, and when you have as it were made them up into one body, let the minds of the English be accustomed thereto."

In worshipping the Virgin Mary, in neglecting the reading of the Bible, and in many other ways the Church of Rome has become corrupted; but enough has been said to show you why, in S. Augustine's time, we were glad to have fellowship with her, but why, in these days, we cannot have communion with her, until she (as the Church of England did at the Reformation) has shaken off her grievous errors, and returned to the purity of the early Church.

In the spring of 597 S. Augustine and his companions landed at Ebbsfleet, in the Isle of Thanet, and sent an interpreter, whom they had brought from Gaul, to acquaint Ethelbert, King of Kent, with their arrival.

He agreed to meet them on a certain day in the open air—by having the interview out of doors he thought the strangers would not be able to exercise magic spells on him! Augustine was most anxious to make a favourable impression on the king, so he carefully arranged his company into a procession, which came solemnly up from the shore chanting litanies. A large silver Cross was carried in front; then came a picture of the Lord Jesus Christ painted on wood, followed by S. Augustine himself, who towered high above everybody, for he was almost a giant, and after him came the choristers and monks.

The king allowed them to sit down and tell him what their errand to his country was, and when Augustine had explained this, Ethelbert answered in a sensible English manner.

"Your words and your promises are very fair, but because they are new and doubtful I cannot give my assent to them, and leave the customs which I have so long observed with the whole Anglo-Saxon race. But because you come hither as strangers from a long distance, and as I understand that what you yourselves believe to be good and true you wish to impart to us, we receive you hospitably and will give you all that is needed for your support: nor do we hinder you from joining all that you can to the faith of your religion."

This was a capital beginning; and the foreigners were then allowed to leave the little island. Only a tiny rill now divides Thanet from Kent, but then the missionaries had to cross a broad ferry to get to Richborough, whose strong Roman walls, which are still standing, must have reminded S. Augustine of his dear far-away home.

Thus they reached the road to Canterbury. Directly the wooden city came into sight, they formed into procession again, with the silver Cross and the painting of our Lord, and the choristers began to sing a litany, ending with the song of praise, "Allelujah." So Gregory's prophecy was already becoming true, and the English land was owning God as its Maker.

Ethelbert gave the Mission a home at Stablegate in Canterbury and they were allowed to worship with Queen Bertha in the old British Church of S. Martin.

You remember how S. Alban was converted by watching the daily life of the priest Amphibalus? So King Ethelbert watched and admired the self-denying holy lives of these missionaries, and then listened to their teaching, and was won over to be a loyal soldier of Jesus Christ. On Whitsunday 597 he was baptized—the first Christian English King.

What a Whitsunday that was for our island! In the North, at Iona, there was the solemn passing away of the saintly and gifted Columba; and at Canterbury, quite in the South, the clever, successful pagan king was becoming as a little child, and entering the Church, the Kingdom of Heaven on earth, by the door of Baptism.

A mighty object-lesson, showing forth the decline of the ancient Celtic Church of Britain, and the new birth of the vigorous Church of England, whose branches are now spreading over every quarter of the globe.

As S. Patrick found in Ireland, so S. Augustine found in Kent, that, when the chief became a Christian, the tribe soon followed his example. Only six months after King Ethelbert's baptism, on Christmas Day 597, 10,000 Saxons were baptized in the River Swale.

Augustine wrote and rejoiced good Pope Gregory's heart with the glorious news. In his turn, Gregory wrote to his dear friend Eulogius, Patriarch of Alexandria, telling him that his prayers for the English nation had been abundantly answered. Queen Bertha, we may be sure, rejoiced too with her now Christian husband, so that many branches of the one Church that Jesus Christ founded sent up their song of thankfulness to Him for the conversion of the English.

King Ethelbert was a truly generous Churchman. He gave his heathen temple to be cleansed and consecrated, and it became the Church of S. Pancras, called so in memory of the boy martyr who laid down his life close by Augustine's monastery in Rome. Then Ethelbert gave up his own royal palace and retired with Queen Bertha to Reculver, that the band of missionaries might have a suitable dwelling and ample space for their noble work.

Near this palace was an ancient British church in ruins. S. Augustine had it restored and named it "The Church of our Saviour Jesus Christ." This was the simple beginning of what afterwards grew into the magnificent pile of buildings now known as Canterbury Cathedral.

Finally, outside the city walls, King Ethelbert gave a piece of land, on which a monastery was built and named the Abbey of S. Peter and S. Paul. These names were soon dropped, and it was called S. Augustine's Abbey. It was used as a cemetery-church, and a sacred library.

Here S. Augustine, King Ethelbert, Queen Bertha, and her good old Bishop Luidhart were buried, and here in the library was stored at least one of the copies of the Gospels that Gregory the Great sent to England in 597.

You can still see these precious Books. One is

safely preserved in the Bodleian Library at Oxford and the other at Corpus Christi College, Cambridge.

Much as we admire Pope Gregory the Great and his devotion to us, yet, through ignorance of the Church history of our island, he did a crying injustice to the ancient British Church.

He never realised that it was still a living branch of Christ's Church, pushed out of England, it is true, but flourishing in Wales and Scotland: and he told S. Augustine that he gave him authority over the Church in Britain. Of course he had no power to do this. The worst of it was, that it caused S. Augustine, instead of having brotherly communication with the ancient Church of the land, to behave in such an overbearing way to her Bishops, that they would have nothing to do with him; so that he lost for ever the chance of becoming "one" with the British Church.

It happened thus. By the help of King Ethelbert, Augustine got the British Bishops to meet him that they might talk things over together. This they seem willingly to have done; but, when they met, Augustine, with "entreaties, exhortations, and rebukes," tried to make them promise to convert the heathen Saxons, who were still going on fighting with the British and seizing their lands. He also wished them to give up their own way of keeping

Easter and of shaving their heads. These latter were only trifling difficulties that with tact would have settled themselves in time.

On the whole the British Bishops seemed to have behaved well under Augustine's trying remarks, but they insisted that they could not give up their ancient customs without the consent of their people, and they desired another synod, or meeting, to which they might bring more members of their Church. This was agreed upon, and the British Bishops meanwhile talked over S. Augustine's proposals.

They first visited a holy hermit, who was held in great veneration by them, and asked him whether they ought to submit to the bidding of these foreign Christians.

His answer was, "If he be a man of God follow him."

"But how shall we know that?" they inquired.

He replied, "Our Lord saith, 'Learn of Me for I am meek and lowly.' If therefore Augustine is humble, you may believe that he has taken upon him the yoke of Christ and offers it to you; but if he is proud, he is not of God and you need not listen to his words."

Again they asked, "How can we find this out?"

"So arrange," answered the hermit, "that he and

his company arrive first at the place where the synod is to be held, and if, at your approach, he rises to greet you, hear him submissively, being assured that he is the servant of Christ; but if not, let him also be thought little of by you."

Armed with this advice the seven British Bishops met the one Bishop of the English at the appointed place.

Alas, Augustine did not show common politeness even and rise to greet them.

They refused therefore to acknowledge him as their Archbishop, for they said, "If he does not rise to meet us, he will treat us still worse when we are under his command."

The meeting broke up stormily. No wonder the Bible bids us "be courteous." Augustine's lack of courtesy had prevented the union of the Churches!

Augustine left the British in disgust and turned his attention towards the Middle Saxons. He easily obtained permission to preach to them, as Sebert, their king, was Ethelbert's nephew.

London, his capital city, had, ever since the Romans conquered Britain, been the largest and most important town in our island. In it were two great temples. One of these was on a hill in the heart of the city and was dedicated to Diana. When King Sebert became a Christian he pulled this down, and on its site he and King Ethelbert built a church, which to this day is called "S. Paul's."

The other temple, dedicated to Apollo, was on Thorneye, "a little island overgrown with thorns and full of reptiles": "a fearful and terrible place, which no one could approach after nightfall without great danger." This temple was also pulled down, and on its ruins rose the West Minster, now grown to our famous Westminster Abbey.

Mellitus, one of S. Augustine's companions, was consecrated first English Bishop of London, and Justus, another companion, was consecrated first Bishop of Rochester.

All went well with the English Church till the death of good King Ethelbert of Kent in 616, when his son renounced Christianity. Sebert of Middlesex died about the same time and left only heathen sons to succeed him. These young men rushed into S. Paul's while Mellitus was celebrating the Holy Communion, shouting out, "Give us of your white bread as you gave our father Sebert."

Mellitus gravely replied, "If you will be washed clean in that saving font, in which your father was washed clean, you too can partake of that Holy Bread."

This did not suit the rude barbarians. They

hated this solemn new religion, and they turned Mellitus and his helpers out of London.

Justus, Bishop of Rochester, joined the exiles, and they fled to France. Laurentius, who after S. Augustine's death became Archbishop of Canterbury, meant to forsake his work too, but a vision which he saw in church the night before his intended departure stopped him. He fancied that S. Peter appeared to him and scourged him for his cowardice. The next morning he went to Eadbald, King of Kent, and told him all about the vision.

It so impressed the king that he resolved to turn over a new leaf. He gave up his wicked life and destroyed his idols: he also sent for Justus and Mellitus back from France. London, however, refused to receive its Bishop, but Mellitus became Archbishop of Canterbury when Laurentius died, and was in his turn succeeded by Justus.

You remember that Gregory asked the name of the king of those Saxon boys who stood in the Roman slave market, and was told it was Alle.

This Alle had a son Edwin, who, after many ups and downs, succeeded to his father's throne and became a famous king. He carried his conquests far north into the land of the Picts and Scots, and the capital of Scotland is still called by his name, Edinburgh, or Edwinburgh.

He sent to ask Eadbald, King of Kent, if he might marry his sister Ethelburga. In answer to this request he was told that a Christian maiden might not marry a heathen husband. Edwin then sent word that his wife should have the fullest freedom in her religion, that she might bring any Christian companions with her, and also that some day he might himself think of adopting her Faith.

So Paulinus, a priest, was consecrated Bishop, and sent with Ethelburga in July 625. On Easter Eve, the next year, the queen had a little daughter, and on the very same day Edwin was wonderfully preserved from death. An assassin, who was sent from the West Saxons to murder him, would have succeeded in doing so had not Lilla, one of the king's chief officers, seeing the murderer draw out a dagger he had concealed in the folds of his dress, put his own body right between him and King Edwin, thus receiving the full force of the blow. So terrific was the thrust that the point of the dagger passed through Lilla's body and slightly wounded the king. Lilla fell dead at his feet, but the wound Edwin sustained soon healed.

These two mercies received by him on that one day softened his heart. He gave his baby girl to Paulinus to be baptized, and vowed that if victorious over the West Saxons he would forsake his idols and serve Christ.

He was victorious, but he still delayed his baptism, saying he must first call together his great men and consult with them.

They assembled at York. The king then asked each wise man in turn what they thought of this new religion.

Coifi, the heathen high priest, was the first to answer. One might have concluded that he, at all events, would have been against it; but his reply showed that he had no belief whatever in the idols that he served.

An aged Ealdorman was next called upon to give his opinion. He knew that before long his life here must end, and evidently he had often sadly wondered what was to come to him afterwards. He spoke earnest words:—

"So seems the life of man, O king, as a sparrow's flight through the hall when you are sitting at meat in wintertide, with the warm fire lighted on the hearth, and the icy rainstorm without. The sparrow flies in at one door, and tarries for a moment in the light and heat of the hearth-fire, and then, flying forth from the other door, vanishes into the wintry darkness whence it came.

"So tarries for a moment the life of man in our sight, but what is before it, what after it, we know not. If this new teaching tell us aught certainly of these, let us follow it."

Coifi then requested King Edwin to allow Paulinus to speak.

Up rose the tall, slender form of Bishop Paulinus, with his dark, handsome face. His words were full of eloquence and truth. As he preached unto them "Jesus and the Resurrection," the aged Ealdorman found the peace he had long sought. Coifi learnt to know a strong, living, loving God he could believe in, and the great Saxon Council of Northumbria agreed to accept Christianity.

Christ must reign supreme—the idols had to be destroyed. Who would do this? "None so fit as I," said Coifi. "I taught the people to believe in them; I will throw them down."

He mounted a charger and seized a spear, both unlawful deeds for a heathen high priest, and rode boldly to Godmanham, where the sacred wood and temple were, made full tilt for the temple door, and split it. Then with the help of the people he burnt the building with its idols.

On Easter Day, 627, Edwin and his chiefs were baptized at York, in a little wooden church he had ordered to be built there. This was the beginning of the glorious York Minster.

Only six years more of life were King Edwin's, but they were years of active work for Christ and

His Church. After his death in battle with that sturdy pagan King Penda, Paulinus fled with Queen Ethelburga and the young princess to Kent.

Paulinus preached well, and converted many, but Northumbria relapsed into heathenism again, because he failed to follow S. Patrick's plan of establishing centres of religious work with the threefold ministry to carry on Christ's Church when he should be called away.

Looking at the Roman Mission to England then, we can only point out the single small kingdom of Kent as having been permanently won to Christ through its labours, and even there Queen Bertha and good old Bishop Luidhart had prepared the ground.

Yet honour is due to S. Augustine for having begun the Christianizing of the English nation, and we thank God that He put it into the heart of noble Pope Gregory to send him to us.

CHAPTER VI

Oswald, King and *Saint*—*S.* Aidan—*Synod* of Whitby—Hilda and Caedmon—Life of the Venerable Bede

"How beautiful upon the mountains are the feet of him that bringeth good tidings, that publisheth peace."

ON the death of King Edwin, the Britons again became possessors of a great part of their ancient property in Northumbria. Their king, Cadwalla, was a most brutal conqueror, who tortured and slew even women and children in his determination to destroy the foreign foe. True, he was only treating them as their ancestors had treated the Britons about a century before, but then the invading Angles had been savage heathens, while Cadwalla was a Christian and knew better.

In this dark time for Northumbria, one of Edwin's nephews, called Oswald, fought for the throne with cruel King Cadwalla, and though his army was far smaller he came off victorious.

Oswald, while an exile, had become a Christian

at S. Columba's monastery on Iona. Before this famous battle began he called his troops round him and ordered a hole to be dug, in which he planted a great wooden cross and held it upright with both his hands, while the soldiers made it firm by filling in the earth again all round it. Then, raising his voice, Oswald called to his army, "Let us all kneel and together beseech the true and living God Almighty of His mercy to save us from this proud and savage foe." They did so, and when at daybreak the fight began, Oswald and his followers defeated and slew the dreaded Cadwalla and his forces.

Oswald was indeed a splendid soldier-king, but it is not his bravery, or his power, that has made him so well known. Like the celebrated General Gordon, the noble Governor of the Soudan, he is most remembered as the loyal, outspoken soldier of Jesus Christ, one who was never ashamed of confessing Him before men.

He found Northumbria pagan: "there was no sign of the Christian Faith, no Church, no altar erected." It seemed as if Paulinus's work had been quite swept away. Oswald sent at once to Iona, the place where he himself had been baptized, for help to bring his subjects into the Church of Christ.

At his request a Bishop arrived, but he soon

returned to the monastery, declaring he could do nothing with the barbarous English.

Aidan, one of the monks sitting by, quietly said, "Was it their stubbornness, or your severity? Did you forget God's word, to give them the milk first, then the meat?"

All turned towards Aidan as he spoke, and he was at once elected as the fitting missionary for the vacant post. He proved to be the right man in the right place. He built his monastery on the little island of Lindisfarne, close to King Oswald's royal palace at Bamborough, and together these two saints of God went forth to convert the heathen around, Oswald acting as interpreter.

With such a king and such a bishop, no wonder that the work prospered. Churches were built and filled with people longing to hear the Word of God: more helpers came from the Scots, and were provided by the king with money and lands to found monasteries.

Bede, the great English Church historian, tells us that Oswald, though so powerful that he reigned over Britons, Picts, Scots, and English, yet ever remained humble and considerate.

He was, one Easter Day, sitting with Aidan at dinner. A silver dish full of dainties was before him, and they were just ready to "bless the bread," that is, say grace, when the servant whom he had appointed to relieve the poor came in suddenly and told the king that a great multitude of persons from all parts were begging in the streets. He immediately ordered the meat before him to be carried to the poor, and the silver dish to be cut in pieces and divided among them.

"The Open-handed" he came to be called from his great generosity, but those hands were not only used in giving, for as Bede goes on to tell us, "by reason of his constant custom of praying and giving thanks to God, he was wont, always, wherever he sat, to hold his hands upturned on his knees."

Oswald's reign was short, it only lasted eight years, but they were years of blessing to his people. He died in battle with that same fierce pagan King Penda who had killed his uncle Edwin nine years before.

This Penda went on with his ravages after Oswald's death. Once he got as far as the royal city of Bamborough, and not being able to take it, as it was built high on a rock, he gathered wood and straw in large quantities, and set them on fire as soon as a wind sprang up which would drive the flames right on to the thatched buildings of the city.

Bishop Aidan on his little island saw the

terrible danger and prayed "See, Lord, what ill Penda is doing." As he spoke the wind changed, the smoke and flame were driven away from the town, and Bamborough was saved.

Old Penda slew five powerful Christian monarchs, but he could not crush out Christ's Church. Everywhere it spread; nay, before his death his own son Peada became a Christian, baptized by Bishop Finan, who succeeded Aidan at Lindisfarne.

In 655 the great battle of Winwood was fought between Oswi, who was then King of Northumbria and Penda. Oswi had tried to buy Penda off, promising him great bribes if only he would leave Northumbria in peace, but the savage old king would hear of no compromise.

"If the pagan will not accept our gifts we will offer them to One who will," said Oswi, and he vowed that if successful he would dedicate his baby daughter to God, and give twelve estates to found twelve monasteries.

It was a fight between Christianity and Paganism, and at its close the terror of all the Saxon Heptarchy lay stiff and dead, and with old Penda died for ever the strength of heathenism in England. You may like to know that Oswi honourably performed his vow in every particular.

But we must return to Aidan, who was grieving terribly over the loss of Oswald. It was a crushing blow to the gentle Bishop, but he went on working for some years longer, preaching, baptizing, confirming, ordaining—faithfully building up Christ's Church.

So respected was he that during his lifetime the question about the time of keeping Easter was not allowed to be publicly discussed, for fear of grieving him, but after his death a great synod was held at Whitby in the year 664 to settle the matter.

Those who had been made Christians by missionaries from Iona kept Easter at one time, and those who had been converted by the Roman mission at another. There was but little difference between the dates, but still it certainly was a drawback that all the English Church should not keep Easter on the same day.

You remember S. Augustine was very angry with the British Bishops because they would not give up their ancient way of reckoning Easter. He need not have been so vexed, as his own way, which is ours now, was, and is still, anything but perfect.

The difficulties of having two days for keeping Easter were, however, specially brought home to Oswi, King of Northumbria, in his own family circle. His queen had been the little baby Eadfleda, who was taken to Kent when her mother and

Bishop Paulinus fled on King Edwin's death from Penda, the terrible king-slayer. Of course she had learnt the Roman way from Paulinus, while King Oswi, her husband, had been taught by missionaries from Iona.

In 664 it happened that on the date when the Scotic Church was celebrating most joyfully the Resurrection of the Lord on Easter Day, the queen and her ladies were keeping Palm Sunday, the solemn beginning of Holy Week. So in the same court and household some members were fasting while others were rejoicing in our greatest Church festival. This state of things could not be allowed to go on.

The Synod, to decide which reckoning was to be maintained, met in the famous religious house of the Abbess Hilda.

On the Scotic side were—	On the Roman side were—
KING OSWI.	KING OSWI'S SON.
COLMAN, Bishop of Lindisfarne.	QUEEN EADFLEDA'S CHAPLAIN.
HILDA, Abbess of Whitby.	WILFRID.

Wilfrid was a clever young priest, who had first been brought up in the school of Iona, but afterwards had travelled to Rome, and had become fascinated by her customs and grandeur.

Colman, on being asked by the king to state his

case, quoted the authority of S. Columba and S. John for his way. Wilfrid replied, "S. Peter has taught the other way;" and he scolded Colman for standing out against all the Churches of the West, and against the command of S. Peter, to whom were given the keys of the Kingdom of Heaven.

"Is this really so," said Oswi, turning to Colman, "has the Lord Christ really given the keys of Heaven to S. Peter? and has S. Columba the same power?" Colman was obliged to say "No" to this last question. Then said the king, decidedly, "I shall do S. Peter's bidding, lest when I come to the gates of Heaven he should shut me out!"

All this was very childish and unlearned, but the effect of the king's verdict was far-reaching and it was certainly a good thing that the Church in England should have only one time for reckoning Lent and Easter, and that she should be in agreement on that subject with the rest of the Western Church.

It was however a terrible trial to the ancient Church of our island, and it was long before all came round to the new plan.

Bishop Colman retired broken-hearted from Lindisfarne with all the Scotic monks, and a good number of English ones, to Iona and Ireland. Saintly men were these, whose lives had been the greatest blessing to the country, though they had differed from the rest of the Western Church in such a trivial matter as keeping Easter a few days earlier or later.

I must not pass from Whitby without telling you of a cowherd the Abbess Hilda had in her monastery there at that time, a rather depressed sort of man who had reached middle life before the wonderful thing I am about to tell you happened to him.

When there was a feast in those days everyone was expected to take his turn in amusing the company. On these occasions Caedmon, for that was the cowherd's name, felt more depressed than ever, for he could not sing or make witty jokes. One night he went to his bed in the stable feeling more than usually stupid and useless.

As he slept he dreamt he saw a heavenly visitor, who spoke to him, saying, "Sing to me, Caedmon."

He answered, "I cannot sing; that was why I left the feast to-night."

"You shall sing to me," the beautiful Being said gently. "You shall sing to me about the Creation."

Immediately, without any teaching, Caedmon began to sing verses to the praise of God; it all came quite easily to him.

On awaking from sleep he remembered all he had sung in his dream: so astonished was he at this gift that he went and told the steward, who was his master, all about it. In a very short while the Abbess got to hear of this strange event, and she sent for him, and in her presence, surrounded by learned Bishops and monks, Caedmon was asked to tell his dream and repeat his verses.

When he ceased relating his experiences all present judged that the Lord Himself had given him this grace. They then read him a passage out of the Bible, explaining it to him, and told him to put it into poetry, and when he had done so to come again and recite it to them.

He left them, and set to work at his new task, so strangely unlike the tending of cattle. The next morning he reappeared with the passage turned into excellent verse.

Then the Abbess Hilda said he must become a monk and leave for ever his homely occupation. He sang, as he was ordered, of the Creation of the world, of the beginning of man and of the Life and Death of our Saviour. Thus Caedmon, the cowherd, became the Father of English Poetry.

Four years after the Synod of Whitby a very celebrated man was made Archbishop of Canterbury, a Greek philosopher and theologian, named Theodore. His birthplace was Tarsus, where, centuries before, S. Paul the Apostle was born.

Theodore was sixty-six years old when he was consecrated Archbishop, but he still had before him twenty-one years of life, and these he spent in solid good work for the English Church. Soon after his arrival in Britain he visited all the island "wherever the tribes of the Angles inhabited." This was the first Archbishop whom all the English Church obeyed.

He increased the number of Bishops, and told every rich landowner that he ought to build a church on his estate for the use of his tenantry, thus laying the foundation of Parish Churches, the Squire's Chaplain becoming the Parish Priest.

When Theodore had finished his tour of inspection; he assembled in 673 at Hertford the first General English Church Council of Bishops and Teachers, at which useful ecclesiastical laws were made.

It was these very Church Councils which by their example led the way to our national Parliaments.

Archbishop Theodore felt very strongly the necessity of education, especially *religious* education. He insisted that every child in the kingdom should be taught the Creed and the Lord's Prayer in the vulgar tongue; while the college he founded at Canterbury sent out clever Greek and Latin scholars.

We owe him a great debt of gratitude for building up our National Church, strongly guarding its independence when the Pope of Rome tried to interfere with its liberties. This occurred in the case of Wilfrid, that clever young monk, who, you remember, was one of the chief speakers at the Council of Whitby, and who had been made, by Theodore, Bishop of the immense diocese of York.

Theodore, in 678, without consulting Wilfrid, which was a pity, divided the diocese and consecrated three more Bishops for the new sees. It was right to have made this division, but it should have been done with tact and gentleness.

Wilfrid refused to submit to the new arrangement, and appealed to Rome, returning from there triumphant with a document from the Roman Court stating that he was to be put back in his old position, and an eternal anathema should rest on the head of him who disobeyed these orders.

This document was read in the presence of the king and wise men, who, instead of being terrified by the threats, were furious with Wilfrid for having dared to invite a foreign court to interfere in English affairs. They took away the document from him and put him in prison for nine months. In time he did get some part of his possessions back, but never what the Pope ordered. Indeed, so little did Theodore think that Rome ought to be obeyed in England, that after this affair he sub-divided the diocese again.

The year of the Council of Hertford, 673, was the year in which Bede, the celebrated historian, whom I have so often quoted, was born. It is wonderful that he should have had the gift of writing so well of the things that were passing around, when the whole of his life was spent in a monastery.

When seven years old he was placed under the charge of Benedict Biscop, abbot and founder of the monasteries of Monkwearmouth and Jarrow. From there he is only known to have once departed, and that was when he went to visit the celebrated Cathedral School of York, which was famous 1200 years ago, and which still exists.

Very fortunate it was for Bede that he had such a master. Biscop, with infinite trouble and expense, had collected a valuable library for his monks' use. Five times he had travelled to Rome and back to secure manuscripts and other precious treasures for his library, the fame of which caused hundreds of scholars to flock to his school at Jarrow.

Bede here was first pupil, and an apt one he must have been, for when he got to be tutor "he taught theology, history, astronomy, meteorology, physics, music, philosophy, grammar, rhetoric, Greek, Latin, Hebrew, arithmetic, and medicine!" He wrote forty-five books and is rightly called "The Father of English Learning."

One of his own scholars, Cuthbert, describes his death in a letter to a fellow-student. It was in the spring of 735. A fortnight before Easter his last illness began. Distressing breathlessness and exhaustion were the symptoms, and his nights were long wakeful ones. Enough, one would think, to make him give up all thoughts of work for others, but it was never Bede's way to spare himself. He still went on lecturing, only saying to his pupils, "Learn with what speed you may, I know not how long I may last."

The lads dearly loved him, and Cuthbert writes, "We wept always while we read." Bede however praised God because he had been so weakened, "for," said he, "whom the Lord loveth He chasteneth."

He was busy on the work of translating the Gospel of S. John into English. "On the day before he died, there was one of us with him, who said to him, 'Most dear master, there is still one chapter wanting, do you think it troublesome to be asked any questions?' He answered: 'It is no trouble, take your pen and make ready, and write fast.'

"Later on, the boy spoke again. 'Dear master, there is yet one sentence.' He answered, 'Write quickly.' Soon after the young scribe announced, 'The sentence is now written.' 'It is well,' he replied. 'You have said the truth. It is ended. Receive my head into your hands.' And thus on the pavement of his little cell, singing, 'Glory be to the Father, and to the Son, and to the Holy Ghost,' when he had named the Holy Ghost, he breathed his last and so departed to the Heavenly Kingdom."

Most truly can it be said of him, "Blessed are the dead which die in the Lord, saith the Spirit, that they may rest from their labours, and their works do follow them."

I wish I had time to tell you of the conversion of the seven kingdoms—how the clever, imperious Wilfrid, when turned out of his bishopric because he refused to have it divided, yet showed that, in spite of his pride, he did wish to serve his Lord, for he went and converted the utterly heathen South Saxons. He found their country in a terrible state of famine, the people so maddened with hunger that bands of men would join hands and leap together from a high cliff into the boiling sea, and thus drown their agonies in death, but Wilfrid taught these ignorant heathen to fish in the sea—before, they had only caught eels in the rivers—and made them cultivate their lands, first, like the Saviour, feeding their bodies, and then giving them the Bread of Life.

Then you would like to hear of the gentle S. Cuthbert in his rocky islet, on whom the sea birds would nestle; or of S. Guthlac, the first English total abstainer.

There was the monk-king, Sigebert, whose people dragged him into battle with a fierce foe, hoping he would save them by his holiness. He would take nothing in his hand but a wand, and fell in the forefront of the battle without striking a single blow.

There were the two royal brothers of the heathen king of the Isle of Wight, who were captured and condemned to death, but were spared at a Christian priest's entreaty, until he had taught them the way of salvation and baptized them. After their baptism they joyfully laid down their young lives in the sure and certain hope of obtaining a heavenly kingdom.

I must not entirely leave out S. Chad, who was so humble-minded that he would always make his long visitations on foot, until Archbishop Theodore himself lifted him on horseback.

The history of Christ's Church in England during these early times is indeed full of thrilling stories of loving self-sacrifice.

That you may be quite clear in your minds about the conversion of the English, I will make a list of the seven kingdoms, with the names of those who, humanly speaking, were the means of bringing them into Christ's Church.

1 Kent, . .	S. AUGUSTINE from Rome.
2 Northumbria,	S. AIDAN of Lindisfarne.
3 Wessex, .	BIRINUS, consecrated by the Bishop of Genoa.
4 East Anglia,	FELIX, a Burgundian, and FURSEY, an Irish monk.
5 Mercia, . .	Four priests from Lindisfarne.
6 East Saxons,	CEDD, sent by Bishop of Lindisfarne.
7 Sussex, . .	BISHOP WILFRID from Northumbria.

CHAPTER VII

The Coming of the Danes—King Alfred—Martyrdom of S. Alphege—Edward the Confessor

"The land was as the Garden of Eden before them, and behind them, a desolate wilderness."

ENGLAND was converted by monks, and so it was no wonder that the country became dotted all over with monasteries and nunneries, houses inhabited, the former by men, the latter by women, who bound themselves to keep for life the three great vows of poverty, obedience, and chastity, and who lived by rule under a superior.

These religious houses were a great blessing to the land in those unrestful times. They were really the only schools, and it was through them that learning and art survived and even flourished. Beautiful specimens of Early English decoration, jewellery, and painting still exist, and some of the books they wrote are among our most prized treasures.

The monks, too, were the only architects and

roadmakers. They were the great protectors of the poor, nursing the sick, and feeding the hungry. But perhaps the best thing they ever did was to teach the people the nobility of honest work, never mind what kind it be; and that even digging or ploughing could be done to the glory of God. They themselves as they used the spade or trowel sanctified their labour by singing psalms and hymns. This was a grand lesson to set before the English, for till they came, work of that kind had been thought degrading, and fit only for slaves.

But a shadow fell, darkening this fair picture of holy simple living.

As the monasteries grew rich and fashionable they gradually relaxed their rules, and at length many of them, instead of being the homes of true religion, became dens of luxury and violence. Even Bede in his time grieved over the change for the worse that had begun, but after his death the state of things became terrible. So shocking did it seem to those who were trying to serve God truly, that when the Danes appeared and ravaged the country, wreaking their fiercest fury on the monks, it was thought a judgment straight from God, and that He was taking this way of purging the land, as, thousands of years before, He had permitted the Flood, when

"He saw that the wickedness of man was great upon the earth."

The Danes were first seen in 778, when three strange vessels, with dragons carved on their bows, approached our coasts. The mayor and sheriff of the nearest town came down unarmed to greet the foreigners as they disembarked, thinking that the ships were stored with merchandise.

But out the fierce Northmen leapt and gave no time for parleying. In a minute the English lay dead on the beach, with skulls cleft by their battle-axes.

After this, whenever a draker, as the Danish ships were called, was seen on the horizon the people became panic-stricken; and about this time a special sentence was added to the Litany: "From the fury of the Norsemen, Good Lord deliver us."

We can imagine the earnestness with which this prayer was offered for help against this terrible mysterious enemy, who came so silently and suddenly, and fell on some peaceful settlement by the seashore or on a river bank, leaving in its place ruin and desolation.

Flourishing villages were reduced to heaps of ashes, and the inhabitants left lifeless and unburied, or carried off by their captors into harsh slavery.

Abbess Hilda's religious houses at Whitby were the first to be attacked by these pirates. They murdered the monks and destroyed the buildings, and filled their ship with rich plunder of gold and silver, Church plate, and embroidered vestments.

On reaching home they told such tales of the stately abbeys still left and the treasures that must be hid in them that more and more ships came over, and for 200 years England was never free from these savage Vikings, or children of the Creek, as the name really means. In the North, in the South, everywhere they came, and in 851 they grew so bold that they actually wintered in the Isle of Thanet.

At Bardney Abbey the same scene of violence was repeated as at Whitby, and all the monks were slain.

At the monastery of Croyland, a brief warning was given by seeing flames arising from burning buildings in the distance. The monks knew then that their hour of doom was close at hand.

The Abbot of Croyland, who must have been a good man or he could not have behaved in the unselfish way he did, hastily collected the most precious treasures of the church and gave them into the charge of the young and strong monks that they might save them and their own lives by flight.

Then, with all the helpless inmates of the monastery, the aged monks and the little lads they were educating in the school, the Abbot proceeded to the church and there comforted their hearts, and prepared them for whatever might be their fate, by praying and praising God, and committing them all to His keeping in life or death.

The Danes had by now reached the sacred building—but they held nothing sacred. In they burst and slew the worshippers. One only child they saved—why I know not; perhaps his beauty attracted them—and took him away for slavery. After four days of terror he managed to escape and find his way back to the monastery. Here the young monks had returned and were busy digging graves for the Abbot and his slain companions.

At Peterborough the same butchery was repeated ; eighty-four monks, with their Abbot, were murdered.

One ray of glory lights up the gloom of those terrible years. It is the martyrdom of Edmund, sub-king of East Anglia. As we read about it we seem to have travelled back to the days of the first ten great persecutions, so like the martyrs of those times was King Edmund in his steadfast confession of Christ under the most agonising sufferings; but the similarity ought not to surprise us, for Edmund served the same Lord and was a member of the same Church as those early Christians.

The Danes offered him his life and kingdom if he would give up being a Christian, but to this suggestion he utterly refused to listen. He was thereupon cruelly scourged and bound to an oak tree, where they made a target of him, wounding him again and again with their sharp darts. He bore it all unmoved, and at last his captors, tired of their sport, beheaded him.

When the persecutors had left, his mourning subjects took his body and sent it away far out of reach of heathen spite. Fifty years later, when the Danes had become Christians, Canute, the Danish King of all England, built a magnificent church to receive the remains of this martyr whom his countrymen had so pitilessly put to death. Both abbey and town are called Bury S. Edmunds, that is, burg or town of S. Edmund, to this day.

It was while England lay thus in misery and desolation that King Alfred was raised up to do a great work for her, and, like good King Oswald of Northumbria, he "went forth in the strength of the Lord God." Even when camping out with his army, he carried his prayer book with him, and the soldiers used to see him reading it by the light of the watch-fires.

You all know the story of his hiding from the Danes, dressed as a peasant and living in a herdsman's hut in a little island of Somersetshire; and the scolding of the cross old woman, who did not know who he was, when he let her cakes burn. Alfred was busy thinking out plans by which to subdue the Danes. Well, if his cakes were a failure, his plans were not, for he came in the spring from that hiding-place and conquered his foes. The result of his conquest was the "Peace of Wedmore," which gave the troubled land rest for ten years.

By this treaty the Danes were allowed to settle in certain portions of England, on condition of their becoming Christian, and King Alfred himself stood godfather to Guthrum, their leader.

Since the monastery schools had been destroyed learning had almost died out of England, and Alfred complained that he could not find one man south of the Thames who knew Latin. So he sent for teachers from abroad, and he himself translated into Anglo-Saxon several books for the use of his people.

He was a good Churchman, too, and did his best to restore the sacred buildings and to preserve friendly relations with other branches of Christ's Church. He kept up friendship with the Church in Rome, and in Jerusalem, and even sent, as far as India, offerings to the poverty-stricken Church there.

King Alfred's life was spent for his people and his name has never been forgotten. This very twentieth century is witnessing a noble statue being raised to his memory: truly "the righteous shall be had in everlasting remembrance."

The last and most terrible invasion of the Danes took place in the reign of Ethelred the Unready, and came as retribution for that monarch's treachery and crime. A treaty of peace had lately been drawn up and all seemed tranquil, when on S. Brice's Day, 1002, by his command all through his dominions a cruel massacre of the unsuspecting and unarmed Danes took place. No rank was spared. At Oxford, where they took refuge in the tower of a church, it was set fire to and all within were burnt alive.

This cowardly and wicked act was terribly avenged by King Sweyn of Denmark and his army. They crossed the sea, and for years marched through the land, burning, murdering, and enslaving the inhabitants. In 1010 they attacked Canterbury. Here the citizens, encouraged by the brave Archbishop Alphege, made a gallant defence.

For twenty days they prevented the fierce foe from entering the city. Each soldier before he took up his post went to the Archbishop to receive his blessing, and to partake of the Holy Communion, and thus cheered and strengthened went forth to his dangerous duty.

Had it not been for treachery within the walls, the city might have been saved. But a monk purposely set fire to a building, and, in the confusion that followed, opened one of the city gates to the Danes.

In a moment all was horror and agony. The brutal conquerors respected no one; women were knocked down, little children were thrown in the air and caught on the sharp spears amid the Northmen's savage laughter, and men were hewn down like trees.

Alphege, the Archbishop, came out and intreated the Danes by their manhood not to make war on babes, and to respect the women. Their reply was to seize him and carry him by force to see his cathedral in flames, and the monks being murdered as they ran out of the burning building. It would have been well for the Archbishop could he have shared their fate, but the Danes kept him alive that they might extort a large ransom from him. The sum they demanded was 3000 pieces of silver, which he could easily have raised by taking the treasures of the Church, but he sternly refused to spend on himself what had been given to God.

He was then put in chains and dragged about

with the army on its tour of vengeance. It was hoped by this plan to shake his constancy and make him give up the Church plate. These seven months must have been a time of overwhelming sorrow to him, for besides the daily misery he himself suffered, there was the awfulness of seeing atrocities committed on his own countrymen which he was powerless to prevent.

One noble work he could do and did, and this must have brought him real happiness in spite of his hard lot. Like S. Peter and S. Paul he brought many of his captors to know the true God and to become members of the Church of Christ.

At one of their drunken feasts the leaders of the army sent for Alphege that they might bully him about his ransom. This was at Greenwich, on the 19th of April 1011. "Money, money, Bishop," they shouted, "we will have money."

The Archbishop stood among them calm and dignified. Death had no fears for him. He still refused to use for his personal deliverance treasure dedicated to God; but he besought them earnestly that they would turn from their evil ways while yet there was time.

They did not relish this kind of talk, and to put an end to it, one of the company took a bone he had just done picking and hurled it at Alphege.

The others thought this rare fun, and more and heavier bones, metal cups, and even stones from the floor, were aimed at him. Thick and fast they came, and at last, wounded and bleeding, the Archbishop fell to the ground, when one of the band, "in cruel mercy," put an end to his long martyrdom by cleaving his head with a battle-axe.

As the brave and gentle Archbishop lay dead before them, even his drunken murderers were awed and allowed loving hands to bear away the saint's body. Later on, when the Danish invasions had for ever ceased and the Christian Dane, Canute, reigned in England, he himself brought S. Alphege's body in solemn procession to his own cathedral in Canterbury.

In 1042 Edward, the son of Ethelred the Unready, was called from his exile to be King of England. Edward was the last of the Saxon kings. He was so holy and gentle that he gained the name of Confessor. He built Westminster Abbey on the site of the church that King Ethelbert and King Sebert had founded 400 years before; and even to our own day people flock to see the famous shrine of Edward the Confessor in the noble building that he raised.

CHAPTER VIII

The Normans—Wulfstan, Saxon Bishop of Worcester—Osmund and "The Use of Sarum"—Anselm and Henry—Death of Thomas Becket, Archbishop of Canterbury—King John and Stephen Langton

"Corrupted from the simplicity that is in Christ."

THE Normans who conquered England in 1066 were at that time a noble race, clever, brave, and very religious.

They found our country still suffering from the desolation the Danes had wrought, and they set about repairing the mischief. They restored the abbeys and brought monks over from Normandy to fill them. Splendid architects they were too, and while the barons built hundreds of great castles all over England, the clergy built churches, always of stone. The cathedrals of Canterbury, York, Durham, Winchester, Hereford, and others, thus rose again, far more glorious, from their ruins.

People who were not rich enough to build

churches themselves did what they could towards furnishing and beautifying those erected by others. The Rev. H. O. Wakeman, in his *History of the Church of England*, tells us of a good man called Ligulf, who lived with his wife somewhere near S. Alban's Abbey. As they watched the rebuilding of the abbey they wished that they had been wealthy enough to give to God so noble a present. But they did what they could. "They sold their flock of sheep and goats, and with the price bought two bells which they gave to the great tower of the monastery church: and when they heard the peals ring out over the hills, and the glad music of the bells call all from far and near to the worship of God, they would say to one another in thankful jest,—

'Hear the sweet bleating of our sheep and goats!'"

Some of the beautiful Norman architecture remains to this day, and for the great improvement introduced into church building they deserve our gratitude. For other things which their coming brought we are not grateful at all. The Pope of Rome had acquired over the Church in Normandy an authority which he had never possessed over the English branch of the Catholic Church. With the coming of the Normans the Pope gained, as might have been supposed, very great influence in English

Church matters, and the English Church, though protesting against such unlawful interference, was gradually trampled on and impoverished by the Church of Rome.

William put Normans into the places of Saxon Bishops, so that at his death Wulfstan, Bishop of Worcester, was the sole English Bishop in the land, and it was only his humility and goodness that preserved the Bishopric to him.

He was summoned to Westminster to give up his crozier or Bishop's staff, and there he declared, "I confess I am not worthy of this dignity"; but the sturdy Englishman was not going to surrender the staff to the Norman intruders. He walked over to the tomb of Edward the Confessor, and laying the crozier there, he spoke solemnly to the dead king these words: "Master, thou knowest how unwillingly I took upon myself this charge—to thee therefore I resign that which I never sought."

An awe fell on the Council, and no man dared move that crozier—a legend indeed says that it clung of itself to the stone. William the Conqueror, touched by the scene, commanded Bishop Wulfstan to retake his badge of office; he did so and ruled wisely and generously over the see of Worcester till his death. The great drawback of having Norman bishops was that they despised the race that had been conquered by their fellow-countrymen, and they were very harsh and overbearing in their manner towards the English.

This state of things caused great ill-feeling, and no wonder. The Norman Abbot of Glastonbury, a wicked man named Thurstan, first starved his English monks and then took away their old chant books that they had used so long, and loved. The monks bore the starving, but not the interfering with their religious books: they rose in rebellion and shut themselves up in the church in defiance.

Thurstan called his bodyguard of soldiers, who rushed up the gallery steps and poured down on the monks a shower of arrows, killing two and wounding fourteen. The monks meanwhile defended themselves as best they could with benches and candlesticks.

You will be glad to hear that the Abbot was sent back to Normandy, but the poor monks also were expelled from the abbey, which was rather hard on them.

One great good, however, resulted from this riot. To prevent such a thing happening again, Osmund, Bishop of Salisbury, collected the best of various collects and litanies that the Church of Christ had used from the beginning. Out of these he made three service books and had them generally used throughout his diocese. To these books was given the name "The Use of Sarum."

They were adopted in many other parts of England, and became the principal service books of the Church for over 400 years. They formed also the groundwork of our present Prayer Book.

As the Pope had helped William the Conqueror to get his throne, he thought he could do anything he liked with him. So he sent his legate Hubert to demand that the King of England should do homage to him, and to the Popes that should succeed him, and that the arrears of Peter's Pence, which he said were due to Rome from England, should be paid.

The purpose of Peter's Pence was to keep up the English college which King Ina had founded at Rome in the eighth century; but by this time the Popes looked upon the money as a tax due to them from England, instead of a gift, as it really was.

William, who probably knew little or nothing about the origin of the tax, said it should be paid more regularly, but he utterly refused to do homage, saying, "I never promised to do it, nor do I find my predecessors have ever done it."

Bishops were mighty princes in those days, so the Pope wished to have the sole power of appointing them in every country, or "the right of investiture" as it is called.

Anselm, a very learned good man, was Archbishop

of Canterbury in William II. and Henry I.'s reign, but he showed too much deference to the Church of Rome, and said it was his duty to receive investiture from the Pope and not the King of England.

Henry declared: "What have I to do with a Roman rule? No man shall remain in my kingdom who does not do homage to me as his suzerain."

The Bishops generally held with the king, and kept up the customs of the English Church. Some of them were sent with a letter from Henry I. to the Pope, in which he declared he would not yield his rights, and that "he hoped the Pope would therefore, on reconsideration, not drive him to the extreme measure of renouncing all intercourse with the see of Rome."

The English Church was constantly resisting the encroachments and exactions of Rome. Pope Paschal II., in 1115, complained bitterly "of the perfect independence of the Church of England." This shows us that the Church of England tried to keep herself independent of Rome *before* the Reformation, as she again became afterwards.

At last the quarrel between Henry and Archbishop Anselm was patched up. Henry gave up his claim to invest with a crozier and ring, symbols of spiritual authority, but retained the oath of homage to himself.

This looks rather as if Anselm had been victorious, but in the end the king got the best of this bargain. He had great influence over the clergy, and before long, when he sent them the "*congé d'élire*," or leave to choose a bishop, he also sent a "letter missive" to tell them whom they were to choose, and they had to obey. The Bishops of the Church of England are still chosen in much the same way.

In 1115 the ancient British Church, called the Church of Wales, joined itself to the Church of England, and promised to obey the Archbishop of Canterbury. The Church in Scotland, and also in Ireland, had already done this, so that now the Archbishop of Canterbury was Primate of the British Isles.

Later on, Henry II. and his Archbishop, Thomas Becket, had a long quarrel too. The question was how the clergy, and people under their protection, were to be judged if they did wrong. For these there were separate courts of justice, in which the judges were bishops and priests, who condemned and punished wrong-doers. Their punishments, however, were very light—perhaps a scourging, or a long fast, or confinement in a monastery. In the king's courts, on the other hand, punishments were terribly severe—branding, cutting off an arm or a leg, or putting out both eyes, were quite common sentences for what we should now call slight offences.

Of course everybody preferred to be tried in the ecclesiastical courts rather than in the civil, and they used all kinds of means to get this privilege. Nor was it difficult to obtain, as the Church claimed the right of judging anyone who had even the meanest work to do in her buildings; grave-diggers, sextons, etc., besides all widows and orphans, crusaders, pilgrims, the poor, and strangers!

The result was that many wicked people did not get properly punished.

Henry II. said the clergy might have the right of trying all these people in the ecclesiastical courts, but should they be found guilty they were to be handed over to the civil or king's courts for punishment. He drew up the "Constitutions of Clarendon" for Becket to sign by way of agreeing to this proposal: Becket had promised to do this, but when it came to the point he refused absolutely to put his seal to them.

Henry II. was right in trying to remedy the evils which he saw so clearly. Yet, on the whole, it was well that the Church in those days had such power, for before there were any Parliaments the kings had almost complete authority, and the Church was the only voice that dared raise itself when they cruelly oppressed the people.

Becket was very obstinate, and Henry was so vexed with him that he had his son enthroned by the Archbishop of York instead of the Archbishop of Canterbury, whose right it was to consecrate kings.

Becket then excommunicated the Bishops who had taken part in the ceremony.

When Henry II. heard of this act of Becket's, he fell into a violent passion, and screamed out, "Will none of my cowardly followers rid me of this rebellious priest?"

Henry did not really mean Becket to be murdered; but four of his knights who heard this speech thought he did, and left immediately for England to do the shocking deed. On their arrival they first went unarmed to the palace at Canterbury and threatened the Archbishop's life if he did not at once remove the sentence of excommunication.

Becket was no coward; he angrily refused, and defied them to do their worst. The knights at once hurried away to get their weapons.

Meanwhile the cathedral bell was tolling for Vespers, and the Archbishop went as usual to the service, in spite of the entreaties of the monks. "At all events," said they, "let us close the great doors of the cathedral;" but Becket would not hear of this. "The church," he replied, "must be open to all;" and he calmly awaited his doom.

In the knights rushed, calling out, "Where is the traitor?"

Becket answered, "Behold me, no traitor, but a priest of God."

They seized him and tried to make him a prisoner, but he set his back against a pillar and resisted them. Seeing they were determined to kill him, he covered his eyes and said, "I commend myself and the cause of the Church to God."

A young monk, called Grim, tried to defend his master, but a heavy sword-blow all but severed his arm from his shoulder. That thrust wounded Becket too, he fell on his knees, and more blows following, he was quickly killed.

All Europe was filled with horror at this murder. Henry II., when he returned to England, did public penance for the part he had in it through his hasty speech. He knelt at Becket's tomb while every one of the numerous clergy of the cathedral (there were eighty monks alone) struck him several times on his bare shoulders, saying, "Even as Christ was scourged for the sins of men, so be thou scourged for thine own sins." Then the rest of that day and night the king had to pass on the stone floor beside the tomb, barefoot, and fasting.

Thomas Becket became one of the most popular of saints.

Thousands of pilgrims came to his tomb from England and abroad. Only a few years after Becket's death an Icelandic chief came and laid a precious offering on it of two walrus teeth, so widespread had his fame become.

Chaucer, the great early English poet, in his *Canterbury Tales*, describes one of these pilgrimages, which reads more like an excursion trip than a religious journey, so jovial were the company.

A grand shrine eventually covered Becket's remains; and Erasmus, who saw it shortly before its destruction by order of Henry VIII., has told us of its magnificence. "Gold was the meanest thing on it. It shone all over, and sparkled and glittered with jewels, which were very precious and rare and of an extraordinary size. Some of them were bigger than a goose's egg. The Prior took a white wand and touched every jewel, telling what it was, the value, and the donor of it, for the chief of them were gifts of monarchs."

We now pass to King John's reign, a time of shame and humiliation for both Church and nation.

The Pope of Rome at that time was Innocent III., who, though a good man, was very ambitious. He refused to accept King John's choice of an Archbishop of Canterbury, and insisted that a friend of his, Stephen Langton, should be elected Primate.

This was unjust both to the king and to the Church of England. It is true that Stephen Langton was an excellent man to be Archbishop of Canterbury, clever, holy, brave, and an Englishman—the very man for those evil times; still, he was thrust unfairly on the nation.

King John was furious and declared that Langton should never set foot in his dominions. The Pope however was determined to have his own way, and he ordered three Bishops to go to John and try and persuade him into obedience. If he still remained obstinate they were to warn him that his kingdom would fall under an "Interdict."

This was the most extreme punishment that a Pope could inflict. When an Interdict was issued it meant that the churches in a country were shut up, no bells were rung, no flesh-meat was allowed to be eaten, and the dead were buried without any religious service. Indeed, the only work the clergy might do was to baptize newly-born infants, and to receive the confession of the dying and give them Absolution.

Even the greatest of all services, the Holy Communion, was suspended during an Interdict.

The three Bishops tremblingly obeyed the Pope's command, and tried to get King John to consent to have Stephen Langton as Archbishop.

John swore he would do no such thing, and that

if any Romish priest dared to publish the Interdict he would put out his eyes; and if any of the clergy attempted to observe it, he would pack them off to Rome and confiscate their goods.

He bade the three Bishops get out of his presence as quickly as they could, as they valued their lives, and they were not slow to obey this command.

On the 24th March 1208, at midnight, the three Bishops nailed up the Interdict on the cathedral door and then fled precipitately to France.

All the Bishops, except the Bishop of Winchester, left the country, but their relations who still stayed in England were imprisoned and the king appropriated all their wealth.

John was too wicked a man to care that there should be no services of the Church; he rather enjoyed the Interdict, for he seized the property of the clergy who obeyed it, and so grew richer and richer.

The Pope saw this, and thought he must do something that the king would feel, so the next year, 1209, he excommunicated John himself, that is to say, no one was allowed to talk to him, or to eat with him, and when he died he would be buried like a dog, for he was under a curse. There was not a man in England bold enough to publish this bull of Innocent III., nor indeed observe it.

The Pope had to think of some other punishment,

so in 1211 he told the English that he had given the crown of England to Philip of France, and was going to help him to gain it, and that therefore they need not obey John any longer as their king.

This was something that touched John at last; he did not like the idea of having no kingdom from which he could extort money, and in which he could gratify his love of cruelty in such ways as starving little children to death, or killing old men by weighing them down with leaden cloaks.

He knew that in the whole of England there was not a soul who loved him; so he feared that his people might take King Philip's side when he came to invade the country.

John was so thoroughly base and selfish that he did not mind the humiliation of England. All he wanted was to secure himself and his own enjoyment. At this crisis he reasoned, "If I submit myself completely to the Pope he will be my great friend and forbid Philip to interfere with me, and I shall still be king."

He therefore sent word that he had grievously offended God, and desiring to humble himself before Him, he gave of his own free will to God, to S. Peter and S. Paul, *and to the Holy Church of Rome, the whole Kingdom of England, and the whole Kingdom of Ireland*, for the remission of his sins. Then, receiving them again from the

Pope, he promised to be faithful and do homage to him.

On the eve of the Ascension, 1213, in the Church of Ewell, near Dover, the Pope's legate sat enthroned, while John knelt before him and laid the crown of England at his feet, putting his hands between those of the legate, and taking the oath of fealty to the Pope as his superior lord.

England had never before sunk so low, and the Church of England had never seemed so completely in the Pope's power as at that moment; but it was John's act alone, and in taking this step he was breaking his coronation oath.

The whole country was overwhelmed with shame. The people murmured, "He is not worthy to be king; he has become the Pope's man."

In less than two years Stephen Langton, Archbishop of Canterbury, who was a patriotic Englishman, in spite of being chosen by Innocent III. had dared to oppose both Pope and king to secure justice and liberty for his oppressed countrymen.

He searched out the old laws and privileges of the kingdom, and found a charter of Henry I.'s. time. Then he called the barons together at S. Paul's, on the 25th August 1213. He explained their rights to them and then told them that they ought to insist on the king's restoring them again.

He made them, in that sacred place, swear to do their utmost to this end. They swore a solemn oath to this effect. Glorious fruits did that meeting bear, for on the 15th June 1215 King John was compelled to sign Magna Carta, that is the Great Charter, which sealed to Englishmen the enjoyment of justice and liberty. The very first sentence that John had to agree to was, "That the Church of England shall be free."

John was obliged to sign the Charter, but he complained to the Pope directly, and as the king was now a dear, obedient son of the Church of Rome, the Pope was very angry about the Charter and said John need not observe it. Moreover, he ordered Stephen Langton to excommunicate the barons who had presented it.

The Archbishop did no such thing. He refused to obey the Pope, thus showing that the Charter was to him, at least, no dead letter, and that he meant to do his best to prevent the Church of England being any longer in bondage to the Church of Rome.

It should never be forgotten that our English liberty, of which we are so proud, is largely owing to the firm stand made by our English Church on this all-important occasion.

CHAPTER IX

Roman Demands resisted by Grosseteste—The Crusades —Wycliffe translates the Bible — Luther and the Reformation abroad — Henry VIII. suppresses the Monasteries

"When Thy Word goeth forth, it giveth light and understanding unto the simple."

FOR over 300 years, however, after the signing of Magna Carta, the English Church was anything but free.

You would hardly believe what she had to suffer from Rome. The Popes persisted in claiming full power over her in consequence of the shameful surrender of wicked King John. They used England as a sort of gold mine to dig money out of. Unceasingly they dug and pocketed heaps of gold.

In 1226 a Pope demanded the pay of two clergy from each cathedral, and the portion of two monks from each monastery in England, to be given to the Church of Rome for ever.

This was refused him, but the English Church

was not always able to hold her own against such mighty sovereigns as the Popes then were.

Fourteen years later, orders came to the Archbishop of Canterbury that no one was to be appointed to the charge of a church until 300 Italians, friends and relations of the Pope, had been provided for in England!

One Italian alone held 700 benefices. Of course he could not look after them himself. These foreigners generally never even lived in the country, but they sent an agent to secure all the Church money, and then paid a small sum to someone to do the services for them.

A good Bishop of Lincoln called Grosseteste was brave enough to preach a sermon before the Pope and his cardinals on this iniquitous practice, and the sore troubles and evils it brought on the English Church. He told them plainly, "The origin of all this is the court of Rome, because it commits the care of the flock to ravening wolves." Later on Grosseteste was braver still in withstanding the Pope, who had ordered him to make his nephew, a mere lad, not even in deacon's orders, a Canon of Lincoln Cathedral.

Grosseteste positively refused to do this, and replied to the Pope's letter in the strongest language: "I oppose these things and rebel against them."

Then he wrote to the nobles and commons of England, warning them that unless they bestirred themselves the Church of their country "which was of old free, will be subjected to a perpetual tribute" to the Roman Church.

Remember, again, that these words were written 300 years before what is called the Reformation, and you will see that that Reformation was not a sudden change, but that the Church of England had long been chafing against the usurping power of the Popes.

When Grosseteste died, in 1253, the Pope asked every true son of the Church to rejoice with him now that his enemy was dead, but the English mourned over the loss of the fearless champion who upheld their Church's rights so nobly.

The Popes had other ways of robbing the English Church. They exacted the first year's income of every clergyman newly appointed to a benefice; and what with fines and taxes, England paid far more to the foreign Pope than she did to her own sovereign.

You have all heard of the Crusades, those holy wars undertaken by Christians to recover Palestine, the land where our Lord Jesus Christ lived and suffered, from the hands of unbelievers? These

Crusades helped to waken people up and enlarge their ideas. They brought the learning of the East into Europe, and universities were founded in various towns, such as Oxford and Cambridge.

About this time, too, the Order of Friars appeared and made a great stir. They were bodies of men who were not shut up like the monks in houses, but went about chiefly in the most crowded cities, teaching the ignorant the true faith and tenderly nursing the sick and dying. At first they proved the greatest blessing to those among whom they lived; but afterwards they became rich by their begging, and then idle, so that at last they were a scandal to religion.

In many of our old cities there are traces of the friars. In Chester, for instance, we have streets called Grey Friars, and White Friars, while in London, Blackfriars has a very familiar sound. Their names came from the variously-coloured gowns worn by the different societies of friars who lived in those places.

Wycliffe, a learned teacher at the University of Oxford, got into great trouble for exposing the vices of the monks and friars, and the corruptions of the Roman Church. He was in danger of his life, but, having friends at Court, he was allowed to retire to his country rectory of Lutterworth.

Here he and his friends worked hard at translating the whole Bible into English. Hundreds of years before, the Venerable Bede, King Alfred the Great, and others, had translated different parts of the Book, but it is to Wycliffe England owes the first translation of the whole Bible; and our present version is not very different from it.

Wycliffe's followers, called Lollards, went far beyond him, preaching rash doctrines and suffering many persecutions.

In 1401 the book of English law was stained by the statute called "*De Heretico Comburendo*," which means "*about the burning of a heretic.*" Christian England was for the first time allowing by law its Christian subjects to be put to death for differences in religious opinions. More than fifty Lollards were burned, the most famous victim being the brave old soldier, Sir John Oldcastle.

One other statute I must tell you about. It is called "præmunire," which is a hard name, but only means to premonish or warn.

This law warned people not to receive any letters (bulls they were called) or gifts from the Pope of Rome without the king's consent. If they did the punishment was exile, loss of property, and imprisonment. This famous law, proclaiming the nationality of the Church of England, was passed in 1393. It showed that the time of Rome's tyranny was drawing to an end.

The invention of printing, which Caxton brought to England from Flanders, was a powerful means of educating the people.

In 1473 Caxton set up his printing press "at the red pale," near the west front of Westminster Abbey. The first books were printed without capital letters and with hardly any stops.

Not only in England, but all over the Continent, people's eyes were being opened to the corrupt state of the Roman Church and the need of reformation.

One way, and almost, if not quite, the wickedest way, the Popes had of obtaining money was by the sale of "Indulgences." Anyone who was rich enough to buy these was promised the remission of all his sins, however great. The sale of these "Indulgences" had begun at the time of the Crusades; but the coarse, outspoken language of John Tetzel, a monk in Germany, as he sold them brought matters to a crisis. He declared that "the souls of dead people would fly from Purgatory to Heaven as soon as the jingling of the money paid for the Indulgence was heard in his box."

This roused the wrath of Martin Luther, the great German reformer. He wrote book after book on the errors of Rome, and thus, more than by anything else, the overthrow of the Papacy took place in Germany.

Our English king, Henry VIII., replied to Luther in a book which so delighted the Pope that he gave the English kings for ever the title of "*Fidei Defensores*" or *Faith's Defenders*, which is the meaning of the letters F. D. that you see on our English coins.

I think the Pope must soon have regretted doing this, for very shortly afterwards King Henry entirely threw him over, and refused to allow Peter's Pence or the first-fruits to be paid any longer to Rome.

He was angry with the Pope for not granting him a divorce from his queen, Katharine of Aragon. She was some years older than he was, and he had got tired of her, and wanted to marry a beautiful maid-of-honour called Anne Boleyn.

But the Pope would not hear of this, and excommunicated Henry, which only made the king more bent on showing himself master in his own kingdom. He put to death sixty-five people altogether for not acknowledging his supremacy, and many more died in prison.

One good thing he did. He ordered that an English Bible should be placed in every church, chained to a pillar or lectern, as books were so valuable in those days. On the other hand, he forbade anyone under the rank of gentleman or gentlewoman to possess one.

Those were cruel times; even children were

tortured if they disobeyed this law. I have read in the *Worcester Diocesan History* of a lad only twelve years old, called John Davis, the nephew of a chemist in that town, who was seized and imprisoned because he had been found more than once reading the Scriptures in English.

He was thrown into a dungeon called the "peep-hole," and here his tormentors used to hold one of his fingers in the flame of a candle, so that the terrible pain might cure him of his wish to read the Bible. He seems to have been steadfast to his principles, which they then tried to shake by a more horrible torture. A raving maniac was shut up with the poor lad in that dark cell! How long he had to suffer this awful imprisonment I do not know. At the Assizes he was brought before the judge and sentenced to be whipped.

From this he was saved by a kind man who took him home with him and tried by gentleness to prevent the boy from reading the Scriptures, but the brave lad withstood this greater temptation.

Luckily for him, and many others, Henry VIII. died just then. We read that John Davis eventually became "a profitable minister in the Church of England."

But the cruellest wrong of Henry VIII.'s reign was the way in which he broke up and pillaged the monasteries and nunneries throughout the land.

The long Wars of the Roses had made some change necessary. Some of them had only five or six inmates, and in the smaller religious houses the rule of living had often been neglected, and careless lives were the result. Cardinal Wolsey, who was a wise reformer, saw these abuses, and suggested to the king that these houses should be suppressed and the monks and nuns should be sent to join the larger monasteries and nunneries, which were properly conducted. This was done, and with the money thus obtained a Grammar School at Ipswich was founded.

So far all was well. Later on Henry wanted money, and he remembered how easily these religious houses had been suppressed and the money diverted to other uses, and he thought he would proceed to deal in the same way with those that were left. So every one that had less than £200 a year was dissolved, and the money was supposed to be taken to found bishoprics, but most of it found its way into the king's purse.

Henry went on from bad to worse. He did not rest till he had suppressed all the monasteries and nunneries, even those which had the most holy reputation and where useful work was being carried on in the education of the young. Such a one was Glastonbury, where at that time 300 gentlemen's sons were being educated, besides poor lads.

He spared, however, Peterborough Monastery, and turned it into a cathedral, because Katharine of Aragon was buried there. He made the Abbot the first Bishop, the Prior, Dean, and the monks, canons and choirmen.

Henry VIII. appropriated nearly all the lands and money and treasures of the monasteries to himself, or else gave them to his friends. He hanged ten abbots, and caused terrible suffering to the monks and nuns by not sufficiently providing for their support. The poor of the land, too, sorely missed the kind help they had always had from these religious houses.

The spoiling of them was done in a wicked, shameless manner, and no excuse can be made for this. Nevertheless, the destruction of the monastic system was a grand thing for the liberty of the English Church, for as a rule these religious houses brooked no interference from the Bishops and owned only the Pope as master; so that their removal saved the English Church from serious trouble and anxiety.

CHAPTER X

The English Church casting away Roman Error—Edward VI. and the Protector Somerset—Queen Mary restores Romanism—Elizabeth again overthrows the Pope's Power in England

"Wash you, make you clean,
Put away the evil of your doings from before Mine eyes."

IN some countries on the Continent the Reformation consisted in the entire separation of the nation, or the greater part of it, from the Church. It is of the utmost importance to observe that this was *not* the case in our country.

In England it was the *Church herself*, gradually casting away error, and going back to the simplicity and purity of the early ages.

In 1516 Cardinal Wolsey reformed the Latin Prayer Book. He ordered the Bible to be read every day, restoring the Lessons, which had been cut down to a few verses, to their original length.

The improvement was greater still a few years later, when these Lessons were ordered to be read in English. The Litany also was translated and was to be sung in churches in the common language: "the goodliest hearing that ever was in this realm."

The translation, however, of the great service of the Church, the Administration of the Holy Communion, in 1548, was goodlier still. A short while before this the Cup had been restored to the laity after they had been deprived of it for three centuries. This refusal of the Cup to the laity in Holy Communion had come to pass through a mistaken idea of reverence.

We are not in the least less reverent, but we carry out our Lord's commands more fully in our service.

The Church of England rightly rejects transubstantiation while teaching in the plainest manner that Christ *is* present in the Holy Communion; though she refuses to try to explain how this comes to pass.

A Real Presence *is* there. "The Body and Blood of Christ are verily and indeed taken and received by the faithful in the Lord's Supper." It is, however, a Real *Spiritual* Presence—"we spiritually eat the Flesh of Christ and drink His Blood; we dwell in Christ, and Christ in us: we are one with Christ, and Christ with us."

In the Holy Communion our Lord does really and truly give Himself to be the food of His faithful people's souls.

Exactly *how* He comes to us then is a deep

mystery which no man can explain. It is one of "the secret things which belong to the Lord our God."

It is said that Queen Elizabeth was once asked to explain her view about the Holy Communion, and she quoted the following verse:—

"Christ was the Word that spake It,
He took the Bread and brake It;
And what that Word doth make It,
That I believe and take It."

The first completely English Prayer Book was issued in 1549. "It was revised in 1552, 1559, 1561, 1604, 1662, since which last date it has remained practically unchanged."

Do not think for a moment that the Reformation gave us a new Prayer Book. It did no such thing. It translated and revised Bishop Osmund's "Sarum Use" that I have already told you about; adding a few beautiful Collects and cutting off the Romish superstitions that had found their way into it: but our Prayer Book is still, in the main, the old service book of the English Church. It contains the prayers of saints and martyrs of the first fifteen centuries of Christianity, together with a large amount of devotional reading taken straight from the Holy Scriptures.

We never can be thankful enough for having such

a priceless treasure-store of prayers and thanksgivings.

Those who have separated themselves from the Church call our prayers formal, because we know beforehand what we are going to say. But a form of prayer does not compel people to pray in a formal spirit; and moreover, Church people, in using Church prayers, have the assurance that they are following a good example, even that of our Lord Himself, who certainly taught His disciples a form of prayer. "When ye pray, say, Our Father," etc.

The great John Wesley wrote in a private letter to a friend, thus:—"To speak freely, I find, myself, more life in the Church's prayers than in the formal extempore prayers of dissenters."

I have heard of an English clergyman who, a few years ago, held a service for some shepherds and labourers in a wild part of Australia.

The church was a wool-shed, and the only light came from preserved meat tins filled with mutton fat, having strips of doeskin for wicks. All this, however, did not matter, as it was the best that could be done in that out-of-the-way place.

It was long since they had had a clergyman among them, and many of the men had ridden miles and miles to attend this meeting. The parson himself always rode with a saddle-bag full of prayer-books, and he now handed them round to his congregation.

Everything went heartily at first, but gradually one voice after another dropped out of the responses, and the clergyman, looking round to see what was the reason of this, saw most of the strong, rough men silently crying. The beautiful, familiar words of the old Prayer Book had melted their hearts. They at least found no formality in them.

In Edward VI.'s reign, 1547-1553, the Church in England gained:—

1. The restoration of the Cup to the laity in the Holy Communion.

2. The translation of the Prayer Book into English.

3. Permission for her clergy to marry.

4. The foundation of about twenty grammar schools and a few hospitals. The Blue Coat School, or Christ's Hospital, was founded then, and the boys still retain the picturesque costume of Edward VI.'s time.

These are nearly all the bright features of that short reign. Unfortunately there is much to record of darker, sadder character. A terrible wholesale robbery of the Church occurred, for which the boy king must not be blamed, as it was the act of his Council. Irreverence of the most appalling kind was rife all over the country.

Who can wonder at it, when the man next in rank to the king, Somerset, the Lord Protector, set an example of the most terrible sacrilege. He actually tried to seize Westminster Abbey and pull it down that he might build himself a palace out of its materials! He was only prevented doing this by the Dean and Chapter bribing him with the immense gift of twenty manors.

Then he turned to S. Margaret's, a smaller church nestling under the shadow of the great Abbey. The parishioners, however, loved their House of God far too well to have it pulled down, and when the masons arrived to begin the work of destruction, they fought so hard and stoned them so thoroughly that the workmen fled in terror. The Lord Protector thought he had better not provoke these brave Churchmen any more, so he left them victors. He went to another part of London and stole two churches and three Bishops' houses, and built his new palace in the Strand with the materials he obtained from these, calling it, after himself, Somerset House.

As I said before, this was not young Edward's fault; he did his very best to prevent it.

The shameful greediness of the Council had taught England that the Pope was not the only taskmaster to fear, so that the people calmly accepted the accession of Mary, the Roman Catholic queen. Of course, under her the Reformation became a thing of the past, and full communion with the Church of Rome was restored.

Mary only reigned five years, and three of these were passed in the most cruel persecution of those whose religious beliefs differed from hers.

Many people had been put to death for their religion since the passing of that hateful Act, "*De Heretico Comburendo*," but England had never before experienced such a time of agony as during Mary's reign.

Two hundred and seventy-seven persons were burnt alive, and amongst these were five Bishops, twenty-one clergymen, fifty-five women and four children.

We have no record of the multitudes who suffered by imprisonment, loss of property, etc. "Seventy-three victims from the city of Colchester alone were dragged through the city of London tied to a single rope!"

At Oxford the two Bishops, Ridley and Latimer, were chained together at one stake to be burned.

Latimer died first. Poor Dr Ridley lingered long, till a bystander in pity, and at great risk to his own life, so arranged the faggots that the Bishop's sufferings were prolonged no further, and both martyrs rendered up their souls to their Creator.

Six months after, Cranmer, Archbishop of Canterbury, was burned at the same spot, where now a noble memorial is erected to these three Bishop martyrs.

Mary's unmourned death, in 1558, put an end to this time of horror; but the remembrance of it sank deep into the hearts of the English, and has caused, more than anything else, that strong hatred of the Papacy which has scarcely lessened during the three centuries that have passed since that reign of cruelty.

When Elizabeth became queen the papal supremacy was again overthrown, and the freedom of the Church of England reasserted. The English Prayer Book was again used in our churches. The Pope himself, it is said, offered to sanction this book if only Elizabeth would acknowledge him as head of the Church in England.

Elizabeth rightly declined to do this; she had already made known her intentions to the Bishops. She told them: "Our records show that the papal jurisdiction over this realm was usurpation. It is by following the proceedings which have come down to me from a long line of predecessors that I mean to rule."

The Bishops who held with the Papacy were deprived by Act of Parliament of their sees, and their places were filled by one Bishop of Henry VIII.'s reign and others of Edward VI.'s reign, whom Mary had driven out. So you see that the line of our Bishops can be traced back without a break to the Apostles' time.

Do not forget this—that the Apostolical Succession of Bishops in the Church of England can be proved to have continued unbroken.

Out of 9400 clergy only 189 were found who objected to the reformed order of things. All the people, whatever their opinions, worshipped in the same churches, and acknowledged the same pastors. There was no schism for many years in England.

In 1570 the Pope, despairing of recovering his authority, excommunicated Queen Elizabeth and her supporters. He declared that her subjects need not obey her, and he gave her dominions to the King of Spain!

On this the Papists, who for the first eleven years of Elizabeth's reign had maintained their union with the Church in England, separated themselves and became a distinct sect.

Thus it will be seen that the *Church of England* has always maintained her continuity, but that the Pope's action put his followers in England into the position of dissenters. Other sects also sprang up about this time, such as the Brownists, Presbyterians, Baptists, sects which are still to be found in some numbers. In the next century all these, with the exception of the Papists, were known by the general name of Puritans.

CHAPTER XI

James I. and the Authorised Version of the Bible—Death of Archbishop Laud and of Charles I.—Cromwell suppresses the Prayer Book—Restoration of Charles II. and the Church's Public Services—James II. and the Seven Bishops—William of Orange and the Non-Jurors

"Approving ourselves as the ministers of God, in much patience, in afflictions, in necessities, in distresses."

TO James I.'s reign we owe our present authorised version of the Bible, which for nearly three centuries has been the joy and comfort of English Christians.

The older translation of Henry VIII.'s time, the Great Bible, as it was called, had been very carefully made; but it contained a few mistranslations, so King James ordered fifty-four of the best Hebrew and Greek scholars to revise it thoroughly; that is, not to make an entirely new translation, but to make the good one already existing better.

So carefully and well did they do their work, that the very cleverest biblical scholars of the nineteenth century, both English and American, when they again revised the Bible in 1884, could not find one blemish "in the least affecting any truth it establishes," although they were able to make many alterations and improvements in the translation.

I daresay you have noticed that the Psalms, as found in the Prayer Book, are not exactly word for word the same as in the Bible. The reason for this is that the Prayer Book Psalms are taken from the Great Bible of 1540. They had been arranged for chanting, and the people had learned to know them; so it was thought a pity to alter the Psalms to King James's translation and thus confuse the unlearned.

The Offertory Sentences in the Holy Communion Service are also from the Great Bible.

James I. was much troubled by the Puritans, who had embraced the extreme ideas of foreign Protestants and Reformers, during Queen Mary's persecution, when they were in exile abroad.

Now the Puritans wished to throw over the Church as well as the Pope, and being joined, as time went on, by the Scotch Presbyterians, and by very many persons who were dissatisfied with the bad government of the Stuart kings, they became at length an exceedingly powerful body.

When Charles I. was reigning they put to death Laud, the earnest and saintly, if unpopular, Archbishop of Canterbury. Four years later Charles himself was beheaded by them.

When the king was in the hands of the Scotch

army he could have saved his life if he would have agreed to the Presbyterian ideas. These ideas included a strong objection to the order of Bishops in the Church. Charles I., however, was right to prefer upholding the institution of his Lord to purchasing his life at such a price.

The Scotch then sold him to Cromwell, who succeeded in bringing about his execution. His last words were, "I go to exchange a corruptible crown for an incorruptible."

Charles had faults, great ones, but he repented deeply of them, and he has, with reason, been called Charles the Martyr, for he was loyal unto death to his faith and to his Church.

Scotland was unhappily not content with expelling error. Led by misguided reformers, she had deserted the one True Church, first planted in her by Columba at Iona. She had adopted as her national religion, Presbyterianism, and to this day Presbyterianism is the established religion of Scotland.

It was a terrible time for Churchmen then. After 1645 people were punished for using the Prayer Book, in any church or chapel, or even in private. If they disobeyed, the penalties were imprisonment and banishment. The jails at once became full of devout, honest clergy.

On Christmas Day, 1657, a party of communicants, who dared to assemble in London to receive the Holy

Communion on that great festival, were surrounded by soldiers and every one carried off as prisoners; think of the loathsome state that jails were in in those times, and you will see this was no light punishment.

Evelyn, who was present, tells us, in his Diary, "as we went up to receive the Sacrament, the miscreants held their muskets against us, as if they would have shot us at the altar."

Cromwell was merciless to the Church. About 8000 of her clergy were turned out of their benefices by him; and he forbade them to hold schools, or even to teach privately, so that many of them were starved.

The following story will show you how great were their privations:—

In the year 1643 a stranger was taking a long winter's walk in the country, and feeling tired and thirsty, he knocked at a cottage door in the village of Bradley to ask for a draught of home-brewed ale.

It was very cold, but as the door opened the kitchen was seen to be fireless, and what was his astonishment to find a clergyman sitting quietly reading a deep book. It was Mr Campbell, late Rector of Swafield, Norfolk, who with his wife and four children had been expelled from their rectory.

He took the stranger to the window and showed

him a little stream a short distance off. "That," he said, "has furnished all we have had to drink for months past, and that is all I have to offer you."

The stranger then asked could he have anything to eat? It is my belief, from his after conduct, that he only asked this question out of kindness that he might find out what the poor clergyman had to live on.

Mr Campbell turned to a disused churn and showed him two or three barley puddings, cold and hard as frost could make them; and that was the only food they had in the house! Bread, butter, cheese, fish, flesh they had not tasted for weeks, neither had they had any fire for a long while.

Even the barley puddings failed in time, and he and his family would have starved outright if this kind stranger had not provided for them till the Restoration.

This clergyman's case, however, was not nearly so pitiful as many.

The Rev. John Cave, his wife and six children, were turned out of home without any notice—not even allowed to take a loaf of bread with them, and the neighbours were forbidden to give them shelter.

Another very learned clergyman was fed for

years on bread and water in a "dire and loathsome prison."

The Rev. Oliver Whitby was shot at while preaching his sermon in Petworth pulpit. He escaped and hid in a hollow tree, and lived afterwards in great want.

They did not stop at plunder and cruelty. They murdered the Rev. Alexander Randall in front of his own house, and then threw the body before his wife, exclaiming, "There's the old rogue, and thou shalt be served the same if thou dost not give us the keys."

You will find these and very many other such sad histories in a book by a Mr Walker, called *Sufferings of the Clergy*. They did indeed prove themselves "Ministers of God in much patience, in afflictions."

The churches, too, were terribly desecrated. When the organ was played in Hereford Cathedral Cromwell's soldiers began to dance in the sacred building. At Winchester they broke open the carved tombs and threw the bones of the dead at the painted windows to break them.

I should not like to tell you a quarter of all the wickedness and ruin they wrought in God's houses throughout the land—it is too shocking to be written down.

Many churches were hurriedly whitewashed to

preserve the frescoes from the irreverent soldiers, and even to this day discoveries are made of these long-forgotten paintings.

For eighteen years the Church of England was silenced, save in one small south-country parish, where our beautiful Church Service was still said publicly every Sunday, the squire of the place being an officer high up in Cromwell's favour and so was able to obtain this privilege from him. The Church of England then was silenced, but not destroyed. In those days the country learned what it was to be without her Bishops and Priests and solemn Liturgy, and to wish for the old days back again, and Churchmen in themselves became wiser and stronger by the purging of affliction.

When Charles II. was restored in 1660 the Church came to the front again too.

Bishop Wren of Ely was released from his twenty years' imprisonment. The Bishops of Oxford, Rochester, Bath and Wells, Chichester and Bangor came from their exile to govern the dioceses from which they had been driven.

The treatment of those men who for many years had usurped the livings, and received the incomes of the clergy who were expelled and persecuted by Cromwell, was very merciful. They were even allowed to retain their posts provided they were willing to be ordained and thus become true ministers of Christ's Church. Some of them had conscientious scruples about being ordained. They very rightly had to give up the livings they had so long unjustly held, for they were not true ministers of the Church, neither did they hold the Faith of the Church.

In cathedrals and churches the Prayer Book was again used, and all save the Puritans rejoiced. They separated from the Church, finding that she clung to Apostolical beliefs about the necessity of Bishops, of Confirmation, etc., and they formed numerous sects.

Oh, how needful, ever since those days, has been that prayer in the Litany, "From all false doctrine, heresy and schism, good Lord, deliver us."

James II. was a Romanist and tried to force Roman Catholics into power, both in Church and State.

He was resisted by the famous seven Bishops whom he sent to the Tower, hoping thus to make them submit. But they were acquitted, and "all England rang with joy" at their release.

After the flight of James II. from England, William of Orange became king. Some of the best among our English Bishops and clergy refused to swear allegiance to him while James, whom they had promised to obey, was still alive. *Non-Jurors* these men were called.

We must respect them, for they patiently suffered great hardships, by losing their sees and livings, for these conscientious convictions.

Still, the loss of such holy and learned Bishops (there were six in all) as Sancroft, Ken, and Frampton was most grievous. After Sancroft's death, in spite of Ken and Frampton's entreaties, the others consecrated new Bishops to continue the succession of Non-juring Bishops, and this succession continued till 1805, when the last of them, named Boothe, who was obliged to earn his living as a medical doctor, died in Ireland.

CHAPTER XII

The Preaching of John and Charles Wesley — The Wesleyans at the Present Time—The Salvation Army—The Church's Care of the Young and Sick and Wandering—The Church founded and preserved by Christ will last till His Appearing

"The God of Heaven shall set up a Kingdom which shall never be destroyed."

MANY years passed away, during which things were smooth and easy for the Church. Perhaps, as a consequence, the Church in England in the eighteenth century became dull and apathetic. She was not without many saintly lives, both among clergy and laity, but also very many of both classes were indifferent and without earnestness.

This is sad to have to write down, but you know the Church of Christ on earth will always be made up of good and bad members; as a family often is of good and bad children. The parables of the field sown with wheat and tares, and of the net full of good and bad fish show us this, and the separation will not be made until the Judgment Day.

England had increased rapidly in population, and the Church made no fresh provision for her children's spiritual needs. Thousands grew up in almost heathen darkness, working, drinking, and sleeping their lives away, without a thought of God.

The Holy Spirit, however, never forsakes the Church. He put it into the hearts of two brothers, who were clergymen, John and Charles Wesley, to rouse up these poor ignorant people. They held prayer-meetings, and preached, telling them how great is the love of God, and how intense the need of repentance and change of life. Their work was blessed, and many souls were rescued.

The Bishops and clergy were at first uncertain about their methods, and were therefore cautious. Afterwards they helped the Wesleys by sympathy and by lending their churches and churchyards for meetings which were attended by thousands.

With success, as is ever the case, came temptations.

The lay-preachers, appointed by John Wesley, began to think that they were as good as any ordained clergymen: they even began to believe that they could administer the Sacraments, instead of continuing faithful members of Christ's Catholic Church, and seeking Holy Orders in the way He appointed.

Wesley became very unhappy about this, and he wrote the following remonstrance to his lay-preachers:—

"Are we not, unawares, by little and little, tending to a separation from the Church?

"Oh, remove any tendency thereto with all diligence.

"Let all our preachers go to church.

"Let all our people go constantly." He also wrote in a private letter:—"We inserted in the first rules of our Society, '*They that leave the Church, leave us.*'"

When Wesley died he was buried, at his own desire, in his vestments as a priest of the Church of England, to show that to the last he remained a member of Christ's One Church.

Unfortunately, Wesleyans have departed far from the wishes of their founder, and have made a new sect outside the Church. We must hope for the day when they will carry out our Lord's will, and return once more to the fold of the Holy Catholic Church.

Except for the great mistake their preachers have made in thinking they need not be ordained by a Bishop, they hold almost exactly the same faith as the Church.

Indeed, until quite lately many good Wesleyans used to deny earnestly that they were at all dissenters from the English Church.

They called their body "The Wesleyan Methodist *Society*," not a Church at all: and they reasoned that they could belong to the Wesleyan Society as well as to the Church; just as you know you can belong to a Temperance Society as well as to the Church.

But it seems that recently all this has changed,

and many Wesleyans profess to believe that their Society can take the place of the Church, and they call their body the Wesleyan *Church*.

The same history belongs to the Salvation Army. It began well by rousing the masses to repentance and change of life, and it loudly declared that it was not intended to form a new sect, but to rescue the outcasts, and then pass them on to other religious bodies.

With success, however, it too became proud, and abandoning its first intentions, made itself into a sect. Salvationists now despise the Sacraments, and have put in their place vain human ordinances. They even view with disfavour the use of the Lord's Prayer.

The waving a flag as they do over an infant is a miserable exchange for the Church's Baptism ordained by Christ Himself.

From all this we see that if once the old paths which God has marked out for us are left, there is no end to divisions and separations.

Year by year the "splits," as dissenters themselves call these new breakings away, grow more and more, though the number of dissenters themselves does not increase.

People who so lightly leave the Church little think what they owe to her, and what they would have been without her.

It was the Church, and *the Church only*, that educated England up to the last century. She began with the monastery schools. Later on she founded the Universities; and later on again hundreds of national schools, where for many years the bulk of the children of working people were educated.

The Church has not given up this, her noblest work, though Board Schools have now been built in many places through the Education Act of 1870.

Every year indeed she raises more than a million of money for the cause of religious education, that her sons and daughters may be brought up in the fear of God and become intelligent members of His Church.

Neither must we forget the large sums of money she spends on the hospitals and charitable institutions of our country, which of course do as much good to dissenters as to others.

I do believe that it is chiefly through want of knowledge that people forsake the Church. So I have written this little book that you may understand what the Church really is—a Divine institution founded by our Lord Jesus Christ, of which He Himself is the Head.

He appointed properly-commissioned officers—the very first being the Apostles. These ordained other men as Bishops, Priests, and Deacons, thus fulfilling the Founder's Will.

Of this Church *every baptized person* became a member at his Baptism.

If he shall continue in the communion of the Church, attending her services, receiving and heeding the ministrations of her officers, the clergy, working for her welfare, he is then not only a member, but a *faithful* member.

But if he has deserted her services and sought other pastors not of God's appointment, thus separating himself from fellowship with the Church, yet he must never forget that by Baptism he was made a member of her, though now an unworthy member.

The Church's officers will, as they are bidden, seek these wandering and straying members: they will welcome back those who have separated themselves, and help them to walk in the old ways, so seeking to accomplish the fulfilment of our Lord's desire, who, the night before His Sacrifice on Calvary, prayed that all His disciples might be *one.*

In striving earnestly for this unity we must not however give up a particle of the true Faith. Remember that no religious body can be a branch of the One True Church that has man for its founder, or which has not the three orders of Bishops, Priests and Deacons continued in unbroken succession from the Apostles.

Saintly men have been found, and are still to be found, in societies which are not the Church—but, as I explained before, every baptized person is a member of the Church though he may not own it, and at Baptism has received God's Holy Spirit.

Above all we must not judge those who have separated from the Church of the Bible, but we ourselves will love and hold fast to her; the closer we keep to her Founder, the more power shall we have of drawing others to the same safe fold.

"Cling fast," says Dr Littledale, "to that great English Communion which offers her children a Liturgy which is pure as well as stately—which holds firmly to the faith of undivided Christendom—which does not lock up the word of God, but reads more of it to her children than any Protestant sect does—which is not ashamed to confess past error and to set about wholesome reforms, and which God has therefore blessed with a marvellous revival — and above all which worships God in Christ."

"I love the Church—the Holy Church
That o'er our life presides,
The birth, the burial, and the grave,
And many an hour besides!
Be mine, through life, to live in her,
And when the Lord doth call,
To die in her—the Spouse of Christ
The mother of us all."

THE END

Colston & Coy. Limited, Printers. Edinburgh.

BIBLIOLIFE

Old Books Deserve a New Life
www.bibliolife.com

Did you know that you can get most of our titles in our trademark **EasyScript**™ print format? **EasyScript**™ provides readers with a larger than average typeface, for a reading experience that's easier on the eyes.

Did you know that we have an ever-growing collection of books in many languages?

Order online:
www.bibliolife.com/store

Or to exclusively browse our **EasyScript**™ collection:
www.bibliogrande.com

At BiblioLife, we aim to make knowledge more accessible by making thousands of titles available to you – quickly and affordably.

Contact us:
BiblioLife
PO Box 21206
Charleston, SC 29413

1629988R0010

Printed in Great Britain
by Amazon.co.uk, Ltd.,
Marston Gate.